Colin Todhunter was born in Liverpool, England and worked at a variety of jobs before uprooting to enjoy a life of uncertainty and travel. He has previously written on a range of social issues and has been published in numerous journals and magazines. These days he concentrates on travel writing and in *Chasing Rainbows in Chennai* has managed to combine a writer's eye and a traveller's soul to produce some lovely and, at times, hard biting accounts of a land where the mundane is mystic and the mystic is sometimes ridiculous.

In 1997, Madras had an official name change. It is now Chennai.

Chasing Rainbows in Chennai

Published in 2003 by Hacktreks, Vancouver, Canada.
Hacktreks is the travel division of Hackwriters.com, Vancouver, Canada.
Email: hackwriters@yahoo.com

This reprint November 2003

Marketed in India by Zine5.com, Chennai.
Zine5 is an online magazine promoting reading and writing. It show-
cases the works of new and amateur writers to wider audiences,
bringing out the writer in every one of us. It can be accessed at
www.zine5.com.
Email: editor@zine5.com

Cover: Egmore Railway Station, Chennai.
Design by Vidya & Navin Sigamany

ISBN   0-9731861-0-0

Printed and bound in India

Chasing Rainbows
in Chennai

- The Madras Diaries -
Traveller Tales From India

Colin Todhunter

Hacktreks Publications

TIL EN ENESTAAENDE REGNBUE
(For a true rainbow...)
LISE

Contents

Foreword by S. Theodore Baskaran

Introduction

1.	Cardboard Cows and Sugarpuffs: A Taxi Ride to Fame	1
2.	Poison Kiss	7
3.	Spaced Out!	13
4.	From Copenhagen to Byron Bay: An Energy Crisis and a Tale of Two Women	20
5.	Chasing Rainbows in Chennai	26
6.	Asian Times	32
7.	Dysentery in Delhi, Chills in Chennai: Don't ask how I am!	37
8.	Out of Chennai and into Madness on the Back of an Enfield	42
9.	All Aboard the Tamil Nadu Express: Next Stop Insanity!	50
10.	The Art of Evasion on an Indian Train	58
11.	Thank God for Sanjay Dutt!	66
12.	Back to the Future on Triplicane High Road	72
13.	Thirteen Hours to Midnight	77
14.	The Point of No Return: Love and Death in India	86
15.	Time Travel on the Road to Nowhere	92
16.	Pancake Overload!	96
17.	Internet India	103
18.	Writers of the World Unite!	107

Contents

Introduction

Acknowledgements

This may be a small book, but it has been a long time coming. It was written on my 11th trip to India, was published during the 12th, and distributed across India during the 13th. Yet, it would have remained in some obscure backwater if it had not been for Vidya Sigamany and Navin Sigamany of the Indian-based publishers, Zine5. Vidya and Navin almost single-handedly published, promoted and marketed the book in India. I would like to thank them for believing in me as a writer and in the book itself. They have put a lot of hard work into this book. Thanks also to the writers Theodore Baskaran for his foreword and Ashokamitran for formally releasing the book at a ceremony at Landmark bookstore in Chennai on May 12th, 2003.

This November 2003 reprint comes six months after the original publication of Chasing Rainbows. Many readers, both Indian and foreign, have provided encouraging feedback during this time, and their comments have been very much valued. However, when a foreigner writes about someone else's country, he or she may unintentionally upset the sensitivities of certain people.

Hopefully, the book will be read in the spirit it was written: an often self-mocking account of one person's inability to sometimes cope with the challenges that India can present. If I have taken sideswipes at India, then my biggest swipes have been reserved for my own civilisation. And if I have said positive things about the West, then my greatest compliments have gone to India.

Colin Todhunter, Chennai, India
November 2003.

Foreword

When I finished reading *Chasing Rainbows in Chennai*, I asked myself what is it that makes Colin Todhunter's writing so endearing? I think it is the ring of authenticity, not only of people and places, but, more importantly, also of his thoughts and feelings. By understanding the power of detail, he manages to recreate and pass on to his reader a feel of the places he has frequented, such as the teashop in Triplicane. Many writers have written on Chennai earlier. Colin Todhunter captures the spirit of the place with ease. This quality, coupled with his style that flows like a stream in the plains, is what characterises his writing.

Often travel writers hurry though a country, stop for short periods, talk to taxi drivers and sit down to write. It is evident that Colin Todhunter takes time to soak in the ambience of the place and time before he writes. This is the secret behind the Big Street of Triplicane coming alive in the pages of this book, as does the atmosphere in an Indian train compartment. Not only places, but individuals too are constructed in living colour. Think of Sach and his short but intense life. This factor endows Colin Todhunter's writings with a credibility that many travel books lack.

In India we come across two kinds of travel writing; one that gives information, may be in a readable format, and the other that is a piece of imaginative prose by itself. It has its own cadence, in addition to echoing the feeling of the author as he journeys from place to place. It is the second category that appeals to me and it is through this kind of writing that the writer is able to share his experience with the reader. Natalie Goldberg, American writer and poet, says in her book *Writing Down the Bones*, that writers live twice, in the sense of reliving their experience as they recall the details when they sit down to write. There is another dimension to this process. By reliving certain moments, they let the readers partake as it were in that experience. Colin Todhunter's work clearly belongs to the second category. This kind of creative travel writing that makes you feel the pulse of a place is rather rare.

In the last two decades travel writing on India has been suffering from a persistent problem: the temptation to cater to New Age aficionados. The purveyors of New Age writing tend to provide a highly sanitised view of India, often ignoring the underpinnings of social injustice that go with it. Colin Todhunter is not under this burden and he is not playing to any particular audience. There is a refreshing quality of transparency in his pieces.

In his introduction Colin Todhunter says, "We are all searching for something. What we seek and what we find can be two entirely different things." May be. But what I found in his writings is something I would like to hold on to.

S. Theodore Baskaran
Chennai, India

S. Theodore Baskaran is the author of The Dance of the Sarus *(OUP, 1999).*

Introduction

You do not need to have been to India in order to appreciate this book. You do not even have to have travelled the world. We are all searching for something. But what we seek and what we find can be two entirely different things. A lot of what is described in this book may be said to be based on an illusion. Many of us are chasing rainbows, hoping to find a pot of gold at the end of them. Yet rainbows are elusive, and along the way what we actually find can be so much more than we ever bargained for.

This book is not intended to be an in-depth account of what India may or may not be. It is written from the perspective of an outsider, and parts of it are about other outsiders or travellers as they pass through. Certain things are glossed over or remain untouched. It was not the intention to describe, for instance, the mystical qualities of the Ganges at dawn, to paint a picture of temple town life in Tamil Nadu, or of marriage festivities in Rajasthan. On the other hand, you may gain insight into other aspects of the country, including the atmosphere inside an Indian gym, the chaos of Indian roads, or the Westernisation of Indian TV.

The stories were all written *on the road*. When I first went to India, some years ago, I suppose that I was searching for something. I do not know what it was, and still don't. But I have found so many things, encountered some amazing people and went to places that I thought never existed - both in India and in my mind!

India will not fail to pour out from the pages, but some stories transcend *India*. For example, *Back to the Future on Triplicane High Road* may be regarded as a personal quest for romantic idealism, in part played out against the activities of a street café in Chennai.

In this book you will meet Sanju in *From Copenhagen to Byron Bay* who attempted to marry-off his sister to me. His utter disregard for compatibility would not make him my first choice for the head of any dating agency. Then there was Sanjay, in *Cardboard Cows and Sugarpuffs*, the neighbourhood hero who I met in a local gym. Mr Sundarjee, the charismatic film producer makes an entrance in *Poison Kiss*. He got me to take a lead role in his film. The fact I had no prior acting experience at all did not matter in the slightest to him. I came across April, who was a little spaced out, and Rudy who was a lot spaced out and a whole host of others who exasperated, maddened and delighted. Even the rich and famous appear in the form of George Harrison, Jimmy Page and Sanjay Dutt. And as you may probably expect from a book like this, there are snapshots of Indian trains, buses, hotels and the usual day-to-day difficulties involved with travelling and living in India.

But there is a lot more than that. The journey will take you to banana pancake hell and give you a ride on the back of an Enfield. It will introduce you to the notion of cockroach *samosas*, talk about the delights of dysentery, ponder the permanency of disillusionment and the disillusionment of permanency, and lead you along the road to nowhere to end up somewhere (maybe).

There is a good deal of love, obsession, tragedy, rejection, and romanticism, all mixed with a dollop of disillusionment and swilled down with a gulp of a sense of loss for good measure. There is even a bit of politics. In *Asian Times* the reaction to the Twin Towers attack is compared with what happened in Bhopal in 1984 when thousands of slum dwellers died in the shadow of the American transnational corporation, Union Carbide. Global TV and capitalism come under the spotlight in the story about *Chasing Rainbows in Chennai*, and the digital divide is briefly discussed in *Internet India*. There is a bit of social and cultural comment, and the final story even offers some inspiration for aspiring writers. I think you will agree, that is a hell of a lot to pack into such a small book!

It is the people who appear on the pages that really make the book what it is. All of them had an impact. Some did so in a fleeting and momentary manner, and others had a lasting and permanent affect. Two people stand out above all others. The story of Sach is presented in *The Point of No Return* and will not fail to touch you. His is one of great tragedy. Sach committed suicide on the Main Bazaar in Delhi. And then there was Lise Kloch from Copenhagen. She burned brighter than the fireworks in Chennai when first I met her on New Year's Eve. She was yet even brighter in the Delhi rain five months later. Lise was a total inspiration, in more ways than she could ever imagine, and remained elusive to the end - a true rainbow.

It does not matter if we cannot keep what we find - at least we once held it, and hopefully gained from the experience before it slipped away. Enjoy the temporary for nothing lasts.

COLIN TODHUNTER

Cardboard Cows & Sugarpuffs: A Taxi Ride to Fame

Travelling through town in a rusting metal box of a taxi in hot pursuit of another gym. No suspension, tattered and torn interior and head wedged against the roof. Every bump and twist magnified from the neck down. Side to side, twisting, turning, avoiding the meandering cows and the potholes. All four windows are open to combat the onslaught of the oppressive Chennai heat. The breeze brings only the noxious odour of exhaust fumes that suck away the oxygen. On the dashboard is a makeshift Hindu shrine; next to it, a stick-on logo which reads *India is Great*. At this precise moment I probably need some convincing. I had little sleep last night during a forty-hour train journey from Delhi. Only five hours late - which isn't too bad. Backpacking across India you get used to it.

The incessant sound of vehicle horns fills the air. Women glide past, perched side-saddle on a thousand speeding mopeds. Their saris drape and flow in the evening pollution, accompanying the strangled wail of film music coming from the street-side shops. We grind to another halt. A million faces wait to cross. Old men in a group pause and peer into the taxi; faces lined from a bygone age, frozen in time with sugarpuff teeth and leathery skin.

"Only five minutes more sir. Very near," the driver insists after another half-hour. He said that ten minutes ago, no doubt he'll say it again in another ten.

After crawling through the traffic for over an hour, I arrive at the gym, nerves shattered and needing to lie down. The gym is one of the myriad concrete buildings that jostle for space, spilling down the hillside toward the road. Outside the door is a massive cow, casually munching on some discarded cardboard. Above the entrance is the hand-painted sign, *Gaylord Gym*.

I make my way in, ill-tempered, jaded and tired from the journey. Why does everywhere seem to be lit with a thirty-watt bulb, I mumble on entering the stairwell. I emerge into the sweatbox and moan, "What? No ceiling fans? No windows?" It is an ugly place with rusting machines and seriously chipped weights. I notice the dust-laden, uneven stone floor and the grimy walls. Fifty people stare in my direction, all in their late teens and each with a look of bewilderment. They've never seen a westerner inside the gym before. Unlike a Western gym, an ethos of hard work is totally lacking and people go through the motions without any real commitment. Taking it easy is the order of the day - the words India and gym somehow don't seem to go together.

As with many places here, the name *gym* is used with a cavalier abandon that would be taken as misappropriation under the auspices of any trades description act. The antiquated contraptions that populate some of these places beggar belief. The only appealing thing about this one is the sweet smell of burning incense. It drifts through the heavy atmosphere from the picture shrine dedicated to Ganesh, which hangs as a centrepiece on one of the walls. Adorned with a garland of bright yellow marigolds, the shrine adds to the special character of the typical Indian gym. The distorted music from the latest film blockbuster is played at the usual ear-splitting level. In front of the shrine is an empty chair and an imposing, old wooden desk, behind which the absent manager or owner would usually sit.

I notice a few fading colour photos of Hindi film stars, cut from magazines and precariously hanging from bits of old tape. Cinema is a religion in India. I see the same faces on walls throughout the country. I recognise one or two; Salman Khan with his classically chiselled looks is the face of the moment. Curiously, female stars rarely make it onto the walls. Indian men seem obsessed with the male stars - especially those who become typecast as the heroes. There are also a few cut outs of champion western bodybuilders with their overblown steroided physiques.

I'm dripping in sweat even before I lie down for the first exercise. The tortuous, metal-backed bench wobbles from side to side. It becomes less a case of me performing the exercise in good style, and more a case of me trying not to slide off. From the corner of my eye I can see everyone gathering. By the time I've got up, they are surrounding me. They form a circle and watch my every move. Fame at last! They probably wonder why I am training so hard, sweating profusely and gasping for breath throughout my workout - after all, it's only thirty-seven degrees outside and eighty eight per cent humidity.

The attention persists for the next hour. I am subjected to the now familiar daily exercise of answering questions about where I live, whether or not I am married, what my job and caste are, how old I am, and so on. On the street, in the hotel, in the restaurant - the same questions, the same answers, four or five times a day, seven days a week.

A big, grinning face peers out from a photo on one of the peeling walls. Someone informs me that this is Sanjay, who will be in later. I am told that I must stay to meet him; everyone agrees. And I agree, not to disappoint.

"When will he be arriving?" I ask.

"Immediately - in one hour sir," comes the reply. It was one of those nonsensical replies that I had become accustomed to.

By now my weariness is overlaid with tiredness, and my belief that anyone who poses as Sanjay does - bare-chested for a gigantic colour poster - has to be an arrogant poser is struggling to show through.

And still the questions go on. What about my training schedules, my diet, how many brothers and sisters, and what do I think of India? Someone asks, "Do you think this gym is good?"

To which I reply, "Well... er... yes. It's one of the best I've been to in India," which is true.

Sanjay arrives and looks as though he has just walked straight out of a Hindi movie. He is over six feet tall, which is unusual for a South Indian. His hair is stylishly combed back, and he's wearing an army flak jacket with upturned collar. Relatively few Indians cultivate such an individual image. To western eyes he may look whimsical, but to the boys he has got it all - the look, the build and the walk. Contrary to my preconceptions, he is very personable.

He sits on one chair and I on another, and we start to chat - the seats had been strategically arranged without my noticing. Everyone in the gym has gathered round to witness this famous meeting of minds. We are the stage act, and they the audience, hanging onto every word. He seems to accept - even expect - a large audience around him. A private conversation for public consumption.

He tells me he has been to the West, and is full of tall tales about his periods in Los Angeles and London. He recalls amusing stories relating to his time spent as a chauffeur, his spell in the state *pen* in California and of the instance when he allegedly beat-up a gang of skinheads single-handedly. I doubt if he actually met any skinheads, but it was an entertaining tale that had the boys listening, laughing and believing.

Sanjay knows all the Hollywood lingo, talking of *chicks* and *pigs* in a thick Tamil accent - a tall man with big stories told in western movie slang and a good wit. He must appear the apotheosis of glamour and sophistication to the boys. Travelling beyond the neighbourhood is an adventure in itself for them.

When I leave, it is like exiting a film set. Sanjay is a blurring of reality and screen-world fantasy to the boys. They hero-worship him; a star performer. And me? - I was probably a strange, exotic character from half a world away. East meets West over a tattered desk in a run-down back street gym. Hardly a world summit, but I bet our meeting was the talk of the gym for days to come.

I hail a three-wheeled auto-rickshaw for the ride back to my hotel. I haggle over the fare.

"Very far, very far. Two hours," the driver insists.

Knowing that it's more like one, I bargain him down. A dozen gesticulations, exaggerated facial expressions and a lifetime later, we agree on a price. I climb in for the long crawl back, further sapped of energy after the mandatory haggling. Even trivial matters are turned into major dramas. We move off and I drift into a semi-conscious dreamlike state. I see cardboard cows eating sugarpuffs, and my picture having replaced Salman Khan's on the gym wall. It's all surreal. Going to the gym was never like this in England.

Poison Kiss

"I would like you to be the main actor in a film I am making, sir."

Everyone in the room turned to see who said this. A few seconds later they began looking in my direction and I almost choked on my coffee. This booming voice from half way across the room had been directed toward me! This was the day I staggered out of bed, and stumbled straight into a movie.

It was a late November day when Mr Sundarjee, an overweight and balding man, approached me over my morning coffee in the hotel reception and asked me - or should I say demanded me - to be in his film. My senses were dazed after a night spent tossing and turning in the heat, but I was soon brought into focus. Mr Sundarjee was the owner of a small film production company here in Chennai. An exceptionally likeable and charismatic man, he explained that he was directing and producing an English dialogue film to be screened in India, parts of Africa and Russia.

Initially, half yawning, I listened out of courtesy. But the more he talked, the less I yawned, and the more I listened with interest.

"I cannot act," I exclaimed. "I have no experience of acting whatsoever."

I couldn't quite believe that he wanted a raw novice. With a typical Indian nonchalance and side to side characteristic head shake Mr Sundarjee replied, "This does not matter. Acting is easy."

I thought to myself, "Yes, bad acting is easy!"

Mr Sundarjee tried to reassure me by adding, "I will coach you on the set."

He went on to explain the script. To my surprise, he was not making a swashbuckling song and dance Bollywood type of movie. My part would be *James*, a softly spoken and dedicated foreign scientist who comes to India to do research on plants that he hopes will earn him a Nobel Prize. James has recently married an Indian woman, Shweta from Calcutta, whom he met while she was holidaying in London. It was a whirlwind romance. One week after their marriage they are in the forests of South India where James is doing his research.

James loves Indian culture and all of its religious traditions, and adores Shweta. Shweta, on the other hand, loves all the *bad* aspects of the West, and is not so sure whether she adores James. James cares passionately about everything, but Shweta cares little for anything. Mr Sundarjee explains that this is a simmering powder keg of disaster. She likes to drink alcohol and sleep around, while he likes to work and thinks he has married a woman who is dedicated to the finest traditions of India. Nothing is further from the truth. She turns out to be his nemesis as the plot thickens into a fog of lust, betrayal and blackmail, leading eventually to the murder of James by their servant and Shweta's lover.

Mr Sundarjee assures me that the film will make international waves. There is only one slight problem, however - a minor difficulty by Indian standards, but one which would slide off the Richter Scale anywhere else. The shooting begins in five weeks and all of the actors are in place - all of the actors that is apart from the two lead roles.

"There will be a small financial renumeration," Mr Sundarjee says almost apologetically. "We cannot afford much as we are only a small production company."

After sleeping on it for a few days, I agree to play the part - or should I say *attempt* to play the part. Five weeks later we are *on location* in the mountains for a twelve day *shoot*. We are in a Kipling jungle-book fantasy land of waterfalls, and fruit orchards. The cool air is sharp relief from the baking, mosquito-ridden plains below. I am playing the part of James. While he works in the forest, Shweta goes into the nearest town each night with their servant for a bucketful of drink and an evening drenched in passion.

Shouts of "action" and "cut" were intimidating, and Mr Sundarjee's frequently furrowed brow was usually drowned in beads of sweat. He always looked to me that he was about to keel over with a heart attack at any second. His worried appearance and chain smoking, however, belied an inner calm.

As promised he was extremely helpful throughout, offering advice and assistance. Every night he would give me my lines, which I would learn, and sometimes fluff the next day. He was a monument to patience. It never took more than a couple of takes to get things right, however. Each scene lasted for no more than forty-five seconds, preceded and followed by a seeming eternity of waiting as the sound, lighting and positions were worked out with meticulous precision. I became acutely aware that patience is an actor's greatest virtue.

The whole film was laden with emotive phrases such as "Your kisses are like poison," and "You shatter my heart into a million fragments." I was saying strange things to a complete stranger, surrounded by other complete strangers. My self-consciousness often showed through, and Mr Sundarjee had to coax me to relax and forget about the camera and crew. He was oblivious to the fact that it wasn't so much the surroundings that were off putting, but his script and the delivery that he desired. He wanted me to say my lines with an exaggerated intonation and distorted facial expression for added effect. I thought that I was sounding false, looking stupid, and that it was all becoming a case of bad film making and poor acting. But he seemed happy enough. I guess he knows his audience and I presume that they like improbable dialogue and over-the-top acting.

Apart from two or three other actors in a scene at any one time, the set consisted of Mr Sundarjee as producer/director/editor, his junior partner, Mr Sooryia, and five assistants who arranged the props, lighting and sound. Mr Sooryia was the sole cameraman. He was also the make-up artist, wardrobe-man, driver and tea maker. Each morning we would suffer a gut-wrenching endurance test as he would drive all of the crew up the bending mountain pass in a battered jeep to our location. On arrival, he would usher everyone out with a prevailing sense of urgency. Then it would seemingly take hours to for him to make the tea and, when he felt like, lay out the wardrobe for the day's shoot. In typical Indian fashion an initial bout of urgency is followed by lingering lethargy, and, on my part, endless impatience and frustration. If we were lucky, the equipment would work first time. But more often than not wires had to be cut, bulbs replaced or clothing re-stitched.

Rabindra, who plays Shweta, is an aspiring big-time actor and hopes the film will launch her to where she wants to be - a Bollywood star. It may well do; she plays her role with poise. She struts around the set wearing tight jeans and listening to hard-rock music, giving James a taster of just where whirlwind romances can lead - in this case, disaster, with James getting more than he bargained for.

The last two days of the shoot take place back in pollution-choked Chennai - which, for the purpose of the film doubles as Calcutta. It's an ideal backdrop for the opening scene as the monsoon skies hang heavy with a sense of foreboding. This is where James meets Shweta's parents after touching down in India. In these opening scenes of the film, Shweta plays the perfect daughter, dressed in traditional attire, and in the role of dutiful wife, providing no insight into the tragedy about to take place in the jungle where she transforms into some kind of bizarre version of a 1970s *rock-chick*.

Much of the shooting appeared to be a kind of organised mess. A film with no stars, a lead actor who hadn't acted in his life, and a rag-tag production crew that seemingly couldn't produce anything if their lives depended on it. In India, people learn to get by with the barest essentials. It was a tale of a battered jeep, some second rate equipment and a third rate actor (me). Yet the near impossible was transformed into the possible, the extraordinary became ordinary, and the high drama of it all turned into daily routine. Somehow I felt we would never get through it, but someway we did. Every day seemed to last forever, and often bordered on drudgery. But the hardship of doing it is now offset by the satisfaction of having done it.

And the name of the film? - I nearly forgot - *Poison Kiss*. I don't know what the finished product will be like, but if Mr Sundarjee has his way, it will be at least passable. And me? - I will return to the UK and drift back into obscurity - well maybe. If you ever pass through Kazakhstan, have a quick look to see what's showing at the local cinema. You never know, Mr Sunderjee's latest blockbuster may be on show. I suppose that now I am *on-screen*, I can travel all over without actually leaving home - a case of always somewhere, but never anywhere.

Spaced Out!

"So, like a bull, my feet are sunk in the soil, laden under a yoke?"

Freedom laughed at my self-assessment. She was a 27-year-old from Sweden who was extolling the virtues of astrology. Freedom had suspected that I was an earth sign by my inability to develop much empathy with fellow travellers in India who are on their own personal spiritual quest. She wasn't blaming me, I'm a Taurean - apparently I can't help it! I plough a deep furrow, with eyes fixed on the ground in a field of my own making. But if I was trapped down on the farm, there were enough people around me who were floating in the clouds.

Like many other travellers, I have been to numerous holy places steeped in mysticism where yoga and meditation courses abound. Unlike other travellers, however, I had never felt any compulsion to indulge in a spiritual quest for inner peace (or whatever it is they search for). You can spot those who do with their talk of *karma, energy, the previous* or *next life, enlightenment,* and of course *ignorance* - the state that anyone who doesn't share their views lives in. For them, everything in India is *magical* or *special,* and nothing is mundane or ordinary. I have nothing against western travellers in India who seek *the truth,* but more than a few fall overboard, and drown in their cocktail of cobbled together beliefs. They are masters of the metaphysical mind game and seek to prove to themselves that they have some significance in an overwhelming universe. Certain chemicals in their brain become rampant, devouring any remnants of sanity.

I had been talking with Freedom in the courtyard of *Broadlands Lodge* in Chennai. Broadlands is a crumbling traveller's institution with a tree-shaded courtyard. Peeling paint and dilapidation are its hallmarks. It usually has more than its fair share of eccentrics in residence at any one time. After Freedom left, Rudy came and sat in the courtyard.

"Don't say that, someone might hear you!" he bellowed.

All I had done was repeated to Rudy what he had just said to me. If he said it, then why couldn't I? There was no one else around anyhow! He told me that he had given away his passport and everything else that he had once owned as part of his spiritual quest. I had said this back to him in disbelief. He was a dishevelled figure wearing a traditional *lunghi* wrapped around his legs. I gave him the address of the French Consulate here in Chennai.

"They will deport me and I don't want to go home. I want to stay in India for five years and my mind is now just about to approach a higher state of consciousness."

14

What could I say to that? What could anyone say? He had nothing, but felt that he was about to gain everything. The next day, I watched him stand outside a shop with outstretched arm, hunched shoulders and begging for money. He reminded me of one of the decrepit dogs that roam the streets of India. There was nothing 'magical' or 'special' about that. He thought that he was walking in the light, but was merely fumbling in the dark.

Not long after Rudy left, another traveller came. Duke was an American in his early twenties. He had long hair and a dangling pointed beard and spoke in a kind of spaced-out (or is that drugged-out?) Californian drawl. After a couple of minutes I decided to break the silence by introducing myself.

"You have just disturbed my *puja*, but I will forgive you this time as you were not to know." He was a fortress of arrogance.

Two other travellers came and sat. Duke was now holding a broadsheet newspaper in front of his face. He suddenly lowered it, said something, and then hid behind it once again. His comment was, "You never know who you are sitting next to in India. I am famous."

The others didn't react. Duke's comments and newspaper mannerisms continued for the next ten minutes. The newspaper was probably some kind of cosmic shield protecting him from my scepticism or should I say, *bad karma*?

He told us that he was famous throughout India, a *swami*, and highly respected by all other holy men across the subcontinent. It all had something to do with his previous life, state of consciousness, or whatever it was he was rattling on about. Duke loved to talk about himself. Each comment seemed more absurd than the previous one.

Then he peaked: he told us that he was the fount of all religious knowledge and that Jesus, Buddha, Mohammed, Vishnu and Shiva all worked through him. Apparently, all of the *Ascendant Masters* (Jesus, Mohammed, Buddha, etc.) were in personal touch with him. He was a legend in his own mind, and talked a lot about living and God. I got the impression that he thought he was a living God. He was lost in space.

He was an inspiration to the two other people present. Paulo and his girlfriend, in their early forties, had been listening intently without saying much. Paulo, an Italian, had been combing his grey beard throughout, while she (French) had been smoking cigarettes through a three-inch holder and occasionally adjusting the black beret which sat on the top of her head. Visually, they were striking.

Paulo looked at Duke. He told him that he actually WAS one of the Ascendant Masters! I looked at Duke. He seemed baffled - even insulted, as it was clear that Paulo hadn't been in touch with him. Paulo was a prophet, no less. He began talking about a revelation that his guru back in France had told him about - although he couldn't reveal it to us. It was something about gloom for the future of humanity if people didn't mend their ways. No surprise there then. Paulo was on a quest. His task was to encourage people to turn toward God. Paulo's face had a constant, pained expression - no doubt as a result of the magnitude of the revelation and the enormity of his mission. He thought that he had the monopoly on suffering. It hung heavy on his shoulders.

His girlfriend then exploded into life. She was scary and ranted that people think too much and rely on the misguided assumptions of science. She said that science cannot explain everything and it is, "The spaces in between thinking where God exists."

Spaced-out thinking I thought to myself - that explained a lot! Really I didn't have a clue what she meant, but I certainly wasn't about to contradict her. I didn't want to put my foot in *it*. But not really knowing what *it* was, I decided to say as little as possible.

I was thrown back into my chair by the force of her conviction. She told me not too think too much, and to have faith in what is unknowable. I disagreed but nodded in agreement, wanting to give the appearance of not being in a state of *ignorance*. She was obsessed (or should that be possessed?). The more she talked, the faster she became. And the faster she became, the louder her voice was. She persisted in repeating herself - as if I was incapable of understanding the first time (maybe she did believe I was *ignorant*). Her voice gradually developed into a screech. She transformed into a screeching parrot before me.

Paulo and his girlfriend rambled on (and on) about God, existence and emptiness, citing dead philosophers from the yellowed pages of yesteryear. The courtyard in Broadlands didn't seem to be a fitting place for them. They needed a grander setting. They were more suited to the Parisian Left Bank of the 1950s, he with his beard, she with her beret and both with their talk of being, nothingness and the bleakness of life.

A Dutch guy called Balance joined us. I don't know from where he got his name. Maybe he had once been in a state of equilibrium, but he had definitely tipped over into his own fantasy world. He was hyper. He was non-stop. Every thought in his head was verbalised. Within the space of five minutes he dominated the gathering and talked about thatched roofs in England, gardening, anarchy, trekking and, of course, God. I couldn't keep up. He was an encyclopaedia of trivia. He had previously been a Hare Krishna devotee, but had fallen by the wayside. He told us that he does not usually drink alcohol, but had two bottles of Kingfisher beer the previous night. Then he went into the local internet cafe and threw-up all over two of the keyboards. They had to be thrown away. They are nice people in the *Gee Gee* internet café and saw the funny side of things. Balance was well known and liked by the local people for his eccentricities. Just as well really.

He then recounted the time he had left his body and had floated through the Parbati Valley in North India, and of the instance when his leg had been broken in Holland, but still managed to cycle to the hospital despite it hanging loosely from half way down his shin. The doctor said that he was not going to treat him as he was drunk (Balance - not the doctor!). So he got on his bike and cycled to the next hospital with leg dangling freely in the night air. I could have put this guy on stage. He was the Dutch version of the American comedian, Jerry Seinfeld. Like Jerry, he didn't tell jokes as such, but just had an endless repertoire of anecdotes. Unlike Jerry however, who deliberately tries to be funny, with Balance it was unintentional.

Perhaps if I lifted my eyes away from the ground, then I could float with these people. A bull, gliding through the air. And pigs might fly. But they were all drunk on their own homemade brands of self-delusion. They were not so much concerned with living, more with the dead. At times, it was like talking to the living dead. Rudy was looking for God. Paulo and his girlfriend had found him. Duke actually thought he was God. And Balance had found him, lost him and was now trying to find him again. I wasn't even looking, hadn't lost him, wasn't trying to find him, but was supposedly surrounded by him everywhere. It was all so deep and meaningless.

Maybe the courtyard in Broadlands was not actually a courtyard at all! Perhaps it was THE farm. It suddenly dawned on me that Freedom had been right. I was indeed trapped. A bull, in the farmyard from hell with an eternity to look forward to of trivial anecdotes and screeching parrots.

From Copenhagen to Byron Bay:
An Energy Crisis and
a Tale of Two Women

"They possess mystical energies and can help to focus your *karma*."

April was convinced that the crystals and gemstones I had bought here in India had qualities that went way above and beyond the laws of natural science. She was a 20-year-old spiritual healer from Byron Bay in Australia. I had been to Byron Bay. It was a hippy hang out where much talk was of cosmic forces and *energy*. A while ago I would have treated any notions of *energy* with my usual cynical disdain as the ramblings of a madwoman who had spent far too much time in India - or for that matter, Byron Bay. But now I wanted to believe because this had been a life-changing trip at a time when I thought life-changing trips happened only to other people.

The first week in late October was spent mainly lying on my bed in Chennai staring up at the rotating ceiling fan. That was to become a regular occurrence. It felt like the end of a trip, never mind the start. I didn't really know why I'd come back to India and was suffering an *energy* crisis from early on. Gazing at the fan didn't help. The stale air wafted around the room, reminding me just how vacuous and hollow things had become. The ceiling fan was sucking me into a spiralling vortex of self-pity. Some people call it a mid-life crisis. Maybe that's what it was.

So I decided to leave the city, and soon found myself sitting on a stone floor in a village house, sipping sickly sweet tea. Sanju, the hotel owner where I was staying had taken me to meet his sister. Asha was studying for a degree, spoke good English and was loyal. After fifteen minutes of hard sell he turned to me and asked, "What do you think?"

I knew what he meant.

"What do you mean?" I replied.

"Do you want to marry?" he said.

She was nineteen. Her mother was one year older than me. I knew nothing about this girl, her aspirations, or personality. This did not matter to Sanju.

"In India first you get married and then you work these things out," he said with amazing casualness.

She was beautiful - the option of months of possible loneliness ahead or a hasty marriage and years of probable regret? I opted for the former and headed back to Chennai to lie under the fan.

New Year's Eve came and I found myself in the hotel reception reading a daily newspaper. Someone sat next to me. She was stunning! She was Scandinavian!! But she looked so out of place, and not like a usual backpacker. It was as though she had come straight from a bar in Copenhagen, dressed in denim jacket, jeans, a tight fitting top and carrying a red shoulder bag. She probably had. She worked in one. She was in India to do research for her studies in social anthropology. We shared something! I had been a social researcher for ten years. We also had another similarity - a mutual distrust of the notion of *energy* and anyone who talked about it endlessly and said they felt it everywhere they went in India. Those people had obviously lost their grip.

We hung out together as travellers do and during a warm January we became friends. But I lost my footing and fell. I couldn't stop falling. The rate of acceleration was frightening, and before I could apply the brakes I had fallen for her. There was a slight snag however - the small matter of that thing called *chemistry*. For me there was plenty, but for her there was none. At school wasn't chemistry something to do with reactions and energies? So I did believe in *energy* after all. I just didn't know it. I needed to meet April in March to show me this. There were also a few other little difficulties - a big age difference, diverging outlooks, and us having almost next to nothing in common. The fact that we were both preoccupied didn't help either - I with her and she with herself, resulting in her complete failure to appreciate my superb qualities as a human being. Apart from all of that, things were going great.

Now to a normal person these things would have been major obstacles, but for someone barely clinging to the edge of reality with their fingernails, they were merely minor setbacks which could (and should) be ignored. Then it struck me - in my desperation I had become just like Sanju with his utter disregard for compatibility. Anyway, we bonded - in opposition. I gave everything but she wanted nothing, and I exuded passion while she displayed indifference. I couldn't stop thinking of her. I was obsessed. The more emotion I gave to her the quicker it drained away. She was a porous pot of a woman.

She knew how I felt. I told her. Splatter! That was the sound of my heart sinking to the floor, exploding on impact and her trampling all over it the instant she told me she didn't feel the same. Mere rejection wasn't going to stop me however. I wasn't about to return to the hypnotic stupor of the ceiling fan so easily. I clung to the desperate belief that if she REALLY got to know me then I was sure she would change her mind. I cared about everything she did. Increasingly she seemed to care little for anything I said.

So the ceiling fan scenario returned. I dreamt of it when asleep and gazed at it when awake. Most of the time I didn't know whether I was awake or asleep. I entered a black hole of ceiling fan syndrome. She absorbed every bit of *energy* I gave. Or maybe it just rebounded. Perhaps she was both an absorber and a repeller at the same time. She was an absorbent repellent!

It was time to make an undignified exit. My crisis was all too rapidly getting out of hand. I escaped to Jaipur, over a thousand miles north in Rajasthan. Distance was to be my salvation - out of sight out of mind, but by that stage I was already out of my mind. That's when I met April.

She was no absorbent repellent. April was a leaking radiator. She leaked warmth and radiated *energy*. April was advising me about buying jewellery to sell back home. She told me that certain stones could answer questions put to them when dangled on a piece of string. I asked for a demonstration, but my request bordered on absurdity. She had to "programme" the stone and that took a lot of time (and *energy* no doubt). I wanted to believe in the hidden power of crystals and gemstones. I needed a vitamin.

April was frightening - in a nice sort of way. She was a heady mixture of Byron Bay hippiedom and Indian mysticism, and spoke of being at one with the eternal vibrations of the universe. I didn't quite know what that meant but it sounded impressive. She talked of witches being burnt at the stake for their knowledge of unseen *energy* and how to unlock it. April was a 21st Century child, but I got the impression that she yearned to live in that long lost age of mystical energy and witchcraft - without the stake burning of course.

April was young and wise, and talked of a higher force and how people had lost touch with its energies. Without it we are nothing and merely exist in our own self-perpetuated ignorance. I could identify with that. April also talked of people you meet who just drain away all of your positive energy. And I certainly identified with that. She was inspirational with her talk of hidden energies and forces, and the astrological powers of amethyst, garnet and a dozen other stones. This was the gospel according to April, who incidentally was born in March.

So I started my own import export business dealing in - you've guessed it - semi-precious gemstones. It was a major life change. I had never sold anything before. I began my trip in crisis, turned into a gibbering wreck, and ended up in May thinking of April, newly *energised* and selling stones. The whole thing felt like a bad dream in a hardware store at times with its ceiling fan vortex, porous pots, leaking radiators and absorbent repellents. I travelled from the coldness of Copenhagen, to the warmth of Byron Bay without ever leaving India. Maybe April was right all along and a higher force had been at work. Perhaps *energy* does exist. If it does, it's a powerful thing.

Chasing Rainbows in Chennai

I had been watching satellite TV in my hotel room for far too long. The more I watched, the wearier I became. The advertisements were almost carbon copies of the ones in the West, in terms of the products and the shiny coca-cola lifestyles promoted. MTV India was populated with veejays (presenters) who talked like Americans, dressed like Americans and probably wanted to be American.

The advertisements and the game shows that interrupted the commercial breaks were exponents of the kind of self-seeking materialism that now all too often passes for entertainment. They even have *Crorepati*!! - India's equivalent of the British prime timer *Who Wants to be a Millionaire*, which in turn was no doubt copied from a similar programme elsewhere. That type of thing is all the rage back home, but watching it in India of all places was just too much. I switched off. I think that the euphemism for all of this stuff is *globalisation* or indeed *westoxification*.

It was almost too depressing to contemplate; but I did, and concluded that we now live in a kind of box that when opened contains a model hand which pulls the lid shut to prevent light from entering and scrutiny of what goes on inside. My friend, Roman, was well used to my deliberations and asked, "What on earth are you talking about?"

I went on to explain that boxes normally contain something that can be looked at. Not this one; it has steel fingers to close the cover. Why be aware of the world's ills and challenge anything when you can live in the dark, drink Pepsi, wear Reebok and shop 'til you drop? We live in a consumer paradise where unfettered desire is a virtue and obsession is the faith. The advertising industry oils the hand that closes the box. Welcome to the nightmare - and we are all invited.

"There is much more to it than what we watch on TV - it's about the type of world we want to live in", I told Roman, but he wasn't impressed. I knew he wouldn't be.

He likes the type of world we live in. He loves *Crorepati, Who Wants to be a Millionaire* and believes that the type of corporate sponsored globalisation now happening is the best thing since sliced bread - even better in fact. Anyhow, he left, looking a little downhearted - no doubt to rest his head in some gas oven after listening to me.

I looked out of the window and wondered where on earth do advertising agencies get their sanitised screen images of urban India from - probably Singapore, with its gleaming skyscrapers, sterile streets, and super deluxe cars. It bore no resemblance to the scene that I was surveying. There were a few dull, grey high rises in the distance; but the street was crammed with disorder - mopeds and auto-rickshaws zigzagging to avoid one another while being pushed out of the way by big, ugly buses. Where were the super deluxe vehicles? But then I realised that *deluxe* vehicles are everywhere in India. In actual fact, the word deluxe is thrown about with carefree exuberance to render its usage almost meaningless.

I have stayed in deluxe and non-deluxe hotels and have travelled in deluxe and non-deluxe buses. In fact, at the lower end of the market deluxe hotels with *homely comforts* are all the rage. Receptions sparkle with cleanliness and cannot fail to impress with smooth marble floors and shiny mirrors. Unfortunately, this facade tends to compensate for rooms that are all too often in varying states of disrepair and decay. Hotel receptions in India never fail to lull me into a false sense of security.

And deluxe vehicles? I have come to conclude that a *super* deluxe bus will most probably get you from A to B with a modicum of comfort; a deluxe vehicle might get you to where you want to be - at least it has a hint of suspension, a semblance of a working engine, and some degree of tread on the tyres; and a non-deluxe one may or may not get you to your destination, having less tread, no suspension and a spluttering engine. And deluxe and non-deluxe hotel rooms? - dusty floors and a dodgy water supply - well the least said the better. Anyway it's all a different world from the one purveyed by the advertising industry. The gap between the glossy world of adverts and reality may be big in the West, but in India it's gargantuan.

Designer labels, lifestyle products and luxury cars? I don't buy into it. Why should I when I can see gold dust sparkling on a floor of black velvet, liquid gold dripping against ebony, and then drift through a purple haze at dusk? What am I talking about? No, I'm not spaced out on LSD. Let me explain.

I always remember my first sight of Chennai. The city lights were spread out on the ground beneath, glowing in the dark as my plane flew over. I knew little about the place but it intrigued and inspired. It was gold sprinkled on black velvet. Years later the place still delights and stirs. I walk along and see earrings dripping like liquid gold against the ebony skin of South Indian women; I look up and see a billion stars shimmering over the Bay of Bengal; and down by the seaside I watch the neon lights and the golden sands of Marina Beach blend into a purple haze as night closes in.

Reality bites, but advertisements suck. In fact, reality lacerates. The sensation cuts deep. It's real, can be grasped and is free! Advertisements, on the other hand, deal in fantasy and create a thirst that can never be quenched. And for those who crave, it's an expensive endeavour. Billions are spent on telling us that somewhere at the end of the rainbow there is a pot of gold. But as day fades to night, the rainbow disappears, and illusion gives way to reality - there is no gold.

There is nothing that can make teeth whiter than white, skin smoother than smooth, and hair shinier than shiny. Wearing the appropriate designer label product will not miraculously turn us into bright, young things. And - believe it or not - drinking the right type of cola will not suddenly make us God's gift to men or women - despite what the happy, smiling faces say. But they want us all to keep on chasing rainbows wherever we live: from Chennai to Chengdu, and from Mumbai to Milan.

I returned to the TV. The advertisements were again in full flow. I was treated to the life-changing wonders of brand named alcohol, coloured fizzy drinks and labelled clothes. Just luxuries that we could do without? No! - they are the necessary, must have, must be seen to have lifestyle products, all because they are endorsed by some beaming cricketer, game show host or Bollywood star. If we do not possess them, then we are failures. If we do possess them, we will feel even bigger failures because by that stage we will have bought into the lie and will be wanting the newer, brighter version of whiter than white toothpaste which we acquired when it was newer and brighter than the previous bright, new version. There is no pot of gold at the end of this particular rainbow, just a bag of rotten teeth.

It's a precarious world we live in, based on hollow myths and promises. But don't tell anyone; it may shatter if people look too hard. It is a fragile invention and because of that, the label on the outside of the box probably reads *Handle With Care*. Maybe it also reads, *Do Not Disturb*, as people bask in their emptiness and watch global TV with eyes wide shut.

Somewhere over Marina Beach in Chennai there is a rainbow, and somewhere over the rainbow there is a new tomorrow. But it's just the old yesterday recycled and sold back to us at a profit. If you chase it you will go full circle and eventually end up back where you started from - standing on Kamarajar Salai (South Beach Road) at dusk wondering what was the point. Then as a magenta mist descends and a black velvet sky closes in, gold will glisten on ebony - and all will be revealed. The best things in life are free. Well, for the time being at least.

Asian Times

In 1970s Britain, when I was a teenager, there was a nightly news programme called *News at Ten*. It was a national institution with massive viewing figures, in a time before satellite and cable TV, and the information superhighway. Millions relied on that programme for their view of the world. Events in Vietnam, Laos and Cambodia were daily news, and South East Asia was the hot spot in the Cold War. Beijing, or Peking as it was referred to, and of course, as now, the Middle East also featured. Those places were on the other side of the world, and I probably could not have located them on a map. I also recall thinking that the year 2000 would never arrive. It was a lifetime away. Twenty five years seemed like a lifetime. When young, even a year can seem like an eternity.

The year 2000 has been and gone, and the world's hot spots have changed - well some of them. Eventually, I not only managed to locate Vietnam, Laos, Cambodia and China on a map, but actually went to those places. I never thought that I would, but I did. I remember standing in Tiananmen Square looking up at the portrait of Mao, thinking to myself that the first time I saw that picture was on *News at Ten* back in 1973 or thereabouts. That was in 1994. It felt a bit surreal. All the more so as a McDonalds restaurant had been built at the opposite end of the square, in full view of Mao. And when New Years Day 2000 came, that felt scary. Time moves fast.

My first recollections of India were in 1984, again through the TV screen, and on *News at Ten*. The American owned Union Carbide factory hit the headlines and I remember an exodus of thousands of people escaping from the poisonous fumes that spewed out from the plant and hung over Bhopal. I visited the city in 1998 and stood outside the main gate of the now closed Carbide factory. Across the road is a slogan that reads *Hang Anderson*, the man in charge of the plant at that time. In front of the slogan is a quite small and humble looking statue of a veiled woman covering her eyes, and carrying a baby. Another child is at her feet. It is a memorial to those affected by that particular outrage. I always remember those TV images of Bhopal. They were awful. I never once thought that I would ever go to India, let alone Bhopal.

More recently, I witnessed the Twin Towers in New York collapsing on my TV screen. I have never been to New York, but I compare the reaction to that event with what happened in Bhopal, and have no doubt whatsoever that the victims or their relatives in New York will fare better than those in

Bhopal. What if Bhopal had happened in America? It would have been a different story. But then again, by its very nature, it would not happen in the USA. That kind of thing is allowed only in the so-called *Third World* (if it can be got away with). Things still drag through the courts. And what has happened to Anderson? You can guess - not a lot.

When I saw the Twin Towers fall down on the British news, I thought that it is better to be a victim in New York than in Bhopal. Both tragedies came from the sky, but a cloud will seemingly forever hang over Bhopal. America's billions will help to ease the pain in New York. Justice is unfair. A dead New York financier carries much more weight than thousands of dead urban slum dwellers. But should any of this really come as a surprise? Sections of the West enjoy unprecedented levels of wealth, three billion live on less than two dollars a day, a fifth of the world's population do not have access to clean drinking water, and local economies are being disrupted by the dictates of Western financiers who control the world economy. All are inextricably linked. The humble rickshaw man in Dhaka, the factory worker in Orissa and the villager toiling away in the fields of Uttar Pradesh have one thing in common - like so many others, they are increasingly labouring under global capitalism.

News at Ten brought the world into everyone's living room. Maybe the quality of news on the TV has got better or worse since that time. I suppose that in some ways it is better. TV stations and companies have mushroomed throughout the world. But how many of them rely on the *BBC*, *CNN* or

Western news agencies to set the agenda or to get their stories from? Now the USA are getting worried because the *Al Jazeera* network in the Middle East dare to set their own news agenda - it is not pro-Western - or to be more precise, pro-American.

The last time I was in the UK, I watched *News at Ten*. It is still going strong. The average British citizen is still subjected to the nightly horrors of the world - but as ever, presented by a reassuring newsreader with lilting intonation and in an entertaining way. Too much gloom, doom and analysis is bad for the soul (and the ratings). I suppose you would have to watch the programme to see the paradox in action. You would probably have to watch much more than that though - the advertisements either side of the news also have the required soothing effect. There is a certain light hearted fizz to it all.

The commercial break is part of the act. What better fizz is there than Pepsi and Coke. They are the ultimate in emptiness with their hedonistic, *Coke is Life, Just Do It,* attitude (both slogans have been used by one or other companies at some time). Their advertisements represent a triumph of blandness over meaning. *Just Do It* implies *Don't think* and *Enjoy!* and has just about as much substance as the air bubbles in a can. Just do what? - I don't know. Who cares? Let's have a Pepsi and settle down for the "news" - public theatre largely void of serious analysis. That's entertainment!

That living room where I watched TV in the 1970s seems a long way away at times. And it is. These days events are not viewed from the cosy armchair of the privileged West in front of the TV. They are not taking place in some far off place that might as well be on another planet. We are all living together - and maybe we will all die together. What once appeared to be a lifetime away in the world of a boy, is only nine hours or so by plane. Didn't Mao once say something about even the longest of journeys having to begin with the first step? Who knows where any journey may lead. Each person has to make his own choice. I know where mine is leading - and it is not to McDonalds in Beijing, Delhi, Mumbai or elsewhere to get a Pepsi or Coke - that's for sure.

Dysentery in Delhi and Chills in Chennai: Don't ask how I am!

Metal beaters from the street below were pounding away with huge hammers, tailors were busy at their sewing machines with sharpened needles, and barbers were scraping faces with cutthroat razors. I couldn't get them out of my head. My brain was pounding, my skull was being scraped and needles were being pierced into the back of my eyeballs. The more I thought of the activities on the street below, the worse I felt.

I stood up; I fell down. I collapsed onto my bed. The fever was agonising, the body pains excruciating, and the vomit and diarrhoea, relentless. In a nutshell, I felt bad, absolutely awful. I had to get to a doctor. I could hardly move. When I moved, my head throbbed - almost to the point of explosion.

My kidneys were on fire and to attempt to lie still seemed to be the least painful option. But I couldn't lie still. I still writhed in pain, and it was going to be fruitless in the long-term. I needed medical help.

It took fifteen minutes to put on one shoe. Bending over was torture; straightening up was more tortuous. I required constant respite both during and after I put on a piece of clothing. It took forty-five minutes to put on the barest essentials, and considering it was forty-four degrees, the essentials weren't much. Then the worst part - leaving my room, going to the hotel reception, and somehow trying to get to a doctor. It all entailed not making a pit stop to the toilet or sink! It was a daunting prospect. A kind of mission impossible.

I felt like hell; I probably looked like hell. I passed a chirpy Australian guy on the verandah in the hotel, "How's it going mate?"

"OK, thanks," I mumbled as I staggered past with head bowed and one hand holding the rail.

I asked the hotel manager to get an auto-rickshaw to take me to the nearest doctor. I was in the Triplicane area of Chennai, and was told that the best doctor was in Mylapore. The thought of being shaken and stirred inside a rickshaw for fifteen minutes did little for me. Anyway, it had to be done. I fell into the rickshaw, fell out of it the other end, and tumbled into the clinic barely able to stand. Before I got into the rickshaw, I thought that I couldn't feel any worse, but after ten minutes of stomach-churning traffic mayhem, I did.

I was shivering, sweating, freezing, and baking. It was non-sensical. I felt like some kind of refrigerated oven.

I wedged myself against a post and a nurse asked if I had a sore throat - just about everything else was sore, except my throat. She persisted in asking me. Maybe she thought that I would finally give in to her badgering and admit to something that didn't exist. But there was a purpose to it all though as I found out later that the only available doctor was an ear, throat and nose specialist. What I needed was a doctor who specialised in raging fevers, burning kidneys, and throbbing heads.

The nurse went away. I clung to the post which was now soaked in the sweat pouring from my hand. In the meantime an impeccably dressed young man, speaking in newly learnt clipped English asked - "How are you today sir?"

I wanted to say - "Just leave me alone." But he looked so proud that he could communicate in English and was clearly trying to impress. It was an effort to raise my head.

"Very well, thank you," I replied.

He expected me to say this - it would be the standard reply that he had learnt from his textbook, and I didn't have the heart to say - "How the hell do you think I am? Go away."

The worst thing about experiencing severe illness when thousands of miles from home and alone, is that it brings with it an acute awareness of personal isolation. No one cares. That's probably not true, but at the time the belief is intense. I know this because I've experienced the feeling on the several occasions that I have been seriously ill in Asia. There is a terrible feeling of helplessness and humility, and it's a humbling experience that I wouldn't wish on anyone.

"How are you?" - is an innocent enough question, which demands a civil answer. But there is a problem. Most times the questioner doesn't actually care how you are. It's just a throwaway phrase, which really means *Hello* - a benign form of greeting. So if this is the case, then why don't they just say "Hello?"

I have no problems with the *Hello* or *Hi* form of greeting. I can just return it with another *Hello* or *Hi*. But if someone enquires how I am, I usually say *OK* or *Very well* - even though I might be feeling depressed, seriously ill, homesick, at death's door or whatever. It's a more demanding and ambiguous greeting. If I told them how I really felt, they would switch off and become bored within seconds. Imagine the scenario: a stranger says, "How are you?" - "Well, I'm feeling down, I've got diarrhoea, the vomits and a terrible feverish headache." Most would probably not use "How are you?" as a greeting to anyone else ever again. In that case maybe I should tell them exactly how I am feeling next time.

I have been sick all over India. I've vomited in Varkala, had dysentery in Delhi and have had the chills in Chennai. And yet on these occasions when some stranger has asked how I am, I have always replied with an *OK* or such like. I don't want to disappoint, or to burden them with my misery, particularly when they seem so perky or have made the attempt to communicate. Even when I have spent the night hanging over the sink throwing up and feel like hell the following morning, I usually oblige with a polite and positive response. Friends are different. I can tell them if I'm feeling bad, but not strangers or casual acquaintances. Well, I now found myself in the local clinic after having spent half the night hanging over the sink throwing up, feeling like hell and having been subjected to a one "How are you?" too many.

Finally, the nurse returned, provided me with a bed, connected me to a drip and gave me an injection. An hour or so later I woke feeling a little better. The pain was now just about bearable.

"How are you?" she asked.

For the first time in a long time, that phrase was a genuine enquiry. And for the first time in a long time I gave an honest account of how I was feeling. For once, there was no ambiguity or irritation. It was a comforting experience.

The next day I was feeling a lot better. I passed the Australian guy on the verandah. He looked ill. His head was bowed and he was staggering along gripping the rail. I spoke but he looked a little irritated, even perplexed. What was his problem? All I had said was the commonly used English acknowledgement, "Alright?"

Out of Chennai and Into Madness on the Back of an Enfield

Steven had two passions in life - motorbikes and rum. Fortunately, he did not really mix the two. He always carried a metal hip flask, which was topped up with Old Monk Indian rum from the bottle shop on Triplicane High Road. But I never once saw him drunk. He had just bought a brand new 500cc Enfield motorbike from a dealership in Chennai, and planned to travel through India on it, ending his trip in Delhi five months later. I could never work out whether foreigners who travel India by motorbike were either brave or mad. These days I am convinced it is the latter.

Steven was a burly Englishman from Yorkshire. He seemed to know everything about bikes. Next to my know-how about them, even a little knowledge would almost qualify as *everything*.

So, to me, he seemed like an expert. I was also impressed by his commitment to safety. He had brought with him from England his crash helmet, and leather jacket, trousers and boots. He insisted on wearing them regardless of the sweltering Chennai heat. From the way he talked, I assumed that he must have had many years experience of motorbiking in England under his belt. After he acquired the bike from the dealership, he eased into things by taking short trips through the streets of the city.

Despite my ignorance of bikes, I used to own one. It was a *CZ* make. It also looked impressive. It was made in Czechoslovakia long before the fall of the Soviet empire and the birth of the Czech Republic and Slovakia. It may have looked good, but it was a heap of junk. It broke down too often, and had all the power of a feather. The Enfield was no different, at least according to Steven. He said that to compare the Enfield with a Japanese bike is like comparing an auto-rickshaw with a Porsche. That may have been a slight exaggeration, but remembering my old CZ, I think I knew what he meant. I asked an old Indian guy who was admiring Steven's bike what he thought about the Enfield. He replied, "They are excellent sir, but they are not very good."

What Enfields may lack in quality, however, they make up for with status. And *doing* India by Enfield is a major achievement for some foreigners. Don't ask me why.

I know all about Indian roads and Indian traffic. Two years ago I once hired a moped and nearly died as I came flying off with Yvonne, my passenger, breaking her fall by landing on top of me. The fault lay with the jeep, which had cut across my path. But that did not stop the police from coming along and demanding cash from me. Apart from that misfortune the rest of my road experience has been gained from taking scores of hair-raising (and hare-brained) trips throughout India by bus. The biggest vehicle rules the roost on an Indian road, and it becomes an effort not to be driven off the tarmac and into a ditch (or into another vehicle). The whole thing is insane.

Every time that I take an overnight bus journey, the roads are clogged with slow moving trucks. The bus driver has a strict schedule to follow. Slow moving trucks and breakneck speed buses do not mix. Whenever I get brave enough to look toward the front of a bus I am in, it is driving at speed and is less than a metre behind the truck in front. It is always the same, so I tend not to look. Then the bus makes a sudden jerk to the right with the aim of overtaking. It makes another quick jerk - this time to the left to pull back in as there is oncoming traffic. After a few oncoming vehicles pass, the driver pulls out once more and goes for it. There is more oncoming traffic. We are on the wrong side of the road. The bus driver has the horn blurting non-stop. The truck we are attempting to overtake slows so we may do so. We pull back in and miss the traffic coming our way by a whisker.

And that is the scenario all through the night. No sleep is guaranteed - not for foreigners - Indians sleep like logs through it all, being well used to it from early childhood. The worse thing is that everyone is at it. Horns blurting, sharp weaves in and out, and this is happening on either side of the road. The last bus ride took fourteen hours to go four hundred and fifty kilometres thanks to the trucks, poor driving and long pit stops to have the bus blessed at road-side temples or for police checks for no apparent reason.

So when Steven invited me to go to Pondicherry on the back of the Enfield, I had a quick rush of blood to the head and accepted. The reason behind my stupidity was that Pondy is only a four-hour or so ride down the coast, and we would be doing it in daylight, so surely nothing could go wrong. I was also impressed by Steven's apparent motorbiking credentials. I will never learn.

By the time the bike was loaded with his gear, it was almost the width of a car. I thought that if he was going to make the thing into some slow moving, sluggish bulk - and given that it was an Enfield, it was already well on its way to being a slow moving sluggish bulk anyhow - then why did he not just buy a car, or take a bus? We started out at seven in the morning to - "avoid the worst of the Madras traffic," according to Steven. He appeared in full battle gear - helmet, leather jacket, trousers and knee-high boots. I appeared in T shirt, cotton trousers and hiking boots. No prizes for guessing who would be the first to end up in intensive care if we came off.

Within ten seconds of hopping on the back, visions of intensive care units came into mind and I knew it had been a wrong move. The Chennai traffic was already approaching mayhemic proportions by that time, and Steven cut right across it with seemingly little thought as we pulled out of the side street and onto Triplicane High Road. It was not so much a case of mad traffic, but insane driving - by Steven. You can usually tell if the driver of the vehicle you happen to be in (or on) lacks confidence, and it was clear that Steven did.

And it became even clearer as we turned left into Pycrofts Road. I used to have fond memories of that road with its silk and *sari* shops. I had spent many an hour there having things made and walking along gazing at the neon shop signs at dusk. With a piece of unfettered driving madness, Steven managed to wreck it all in one fell swoop. A slow moving metal hulk of a bus blocked our path. Instead of sitting in and waiting for it to accelerate, he pulls out with his slow moving metal hulk of a bike heading straight into the path of an oncoming auto-rickshaw. He then pulls even further out to the wrong side of the road to avoid it. At that stage, we were where the pavement should be (if one had existed) on the opposite side of the road, weaving between a telegraph post and an unsuspecting pedestrian. We had not been gone for more than two minutes and my heart had been in my mouth twice. And that is where it remained.

We crawled along South Beach Road and into Mylapore. Steven's confidence was not improving. In fact, I could feel it worsening with each close encounter. Still in Chennai, some fifteen minutes later, Steven decided that it was time for another near-death experience. Yet again, there is a bus, but this time he decides to overtake on the inside. There was no road. This did not matter to Steven. Once again, but this time through free choice, he went onto what passes for a pavement. We are racing between posts that hold up a verandah and emerge into a crossroad junction just ahead of the bus, and carry on regardless of any consideration for right of way issues. Unbelievable. But we make it in one piece. Later he told me that he felt the air current from the bus against his leg as we managed to miss it my what must have been millimetres.

A few minutes later, we are lost. We pull over to ask someone for directions. We want the main road to Pondy. The pedestrian seems to understand us. He holds his arm aloft and waves his hand freely. We need him to be more precise. His arm is pointing slightly in one direction, but the hand on the end of it is waving about in a directionless manner. But I am used to this. Whenever I get lost on an Indian street and ask someone to point me in a certain direction, a similar arm and hand gesture ensues. What it means is "Somewhere else; not here." The person hasn't a clue about where it is that we want - only that it is not here. Obviously he thinks that he is being extremely helpful, and that we would never have guessed that the place we require is "not here." We thank him for his expert knowledge of the city, move off and find the road - eventually.

Apparently, the staff in the dealership had told Steven if he was involved in an accident then he should not stop - or at least get back on (if able) and drive off. The reasoning behind this was that no matter whose fault it may have been, as a foreigner, demands for a large wad of money would be made by the gathering crowd - and have no doubt, a gathering crowd there would be. I knew this from my accident two years back.

It was good advice for as soon as we get into the countryside we hit a pedestrian. It is not our fault - honest! He is an old guy who walks out across the road totally oblivious to the fact he is actually on a road. He keeps walking to the right. Steven begins steering to the right. He carries on to the right and so do we. It gets to the point where Steven thinks the guy must surely wake up and turn back and go to the left, so we cannot really afford to take the risk of veering left. The inevitable happens. Steven's protruding luggage clips him. We shake but manage to stay upright. He falls and lands on the floor. Steven sees him in the mirror, on his backside, shaking his sandal in our direction.

Well, that was enough for me. Pondicherry cannot come quick enough. Pondy is unusual for an Indian city. It is planned and has a central grid system. Unfortunately, this makes for a convoluted and confusing array of one-way systems. So we have to make numerous right angled turns on this tank of a bike. In order to complete such sharp turns, the bike almost comes to a stop. Just when I am convinced we are about to fall completely over, the bike picks up speed, completes the turn and returns to an upright position. The turns go on forever - until we manage to find our designated hotel.

What a performance. In the hotel, Steven tells me he has only been driving for two years. Bang goes the veteran status I accorded him. He also tells me that back in the UK he rides thirty kilometres to and from work each day and has at least three near misses per day. And that is on the relative safety of

British roads. So much for his apparent commitment to safety issues.

Two days later he asks if I want to continue with him on his next leg to Mysore - a much more serious undertaking than the Chennai to Pondy route. Steven justifies his reckless driving (which he of course did not regard as reckless) by saying that Indian drivers will drive you off the road if you do not stand your ground. His philosophy seemed to be to try to drive them off the road first. Not a good idea on a motorbike. I take the bus back to Chennai. Reckless driving is better experienced from the comfort of a passenger seat in a bus rather than from the back seat of a bike.

All Aboard the Tamil Nadu Express:
Next Stop, Insanity!
(Or *Split Down the Middle*)

It was a rock and roll journey in India. Well, sort of; except there was no actual music playing, little travelling involved, and it could have taken place almost anywhere - it just happened to be in India. I was a long-term inmate (or should that be resident) of *Broadlands Lodge* in Chennai. I checked in and couldn't be bothered to check out. During my stay I met a guy. He was a writer or something. I felt that somehow I already knew him.

"Have you ever noticed when you order a drink in a café that the waiter asks how many? There is only me sitting there. How many does he think I want?"

He was full of anecdotes about the nuances of Indian cafes and restaurants.

"And when he brings the bottle over, he gives you a blank stare and asks - open? Like I'm going to sit there looking at it or bite the top off myself with my teeth."

The way this guy was ad-libbing, he could have been a stage act.

"What about the waiters? These places are all over-staffed. If you are lucky you may attract their attention because usually they just stand around waiting. If you can get them to place your order, you wait an eternity for them to bring it. In fact, you are the waiter, not them!"

He was an expert complainer, and was convinced that the notion of *customer service* was alien to India. He told me that he had met a woman in the hotel, and was absolutely crazy about her. The moment he saw her he knew that she was a heartbreaker. He said that's when Jimmy Page's mind-blowing guitar riff began playing inside of his head with Robert Plant screaming *Heartbreaker* over it (I thought to myself - WHAT!?). He swore that if that classic Led Zeppelin track had not already existed, he would have penned it the instant he set eyes on her. He couldn't write music nor play any musical instruments - but he was deadly serious.

I knew the girl in question, and yes - she was a stunner and maybe could, would and did break hearts. But, in all probability, if she did, it would not be her fault. It was easy to see why some could fall for her, but if she didn't feel the same then it would be a sorry tale of heartbreak. She turned out to be inspirational - but in a bad sort of way.

I could just about handle the first *head song* and take it as a joke, but soon I began to get worried. I no longer believed the situation to be just different; I was now convinced that it was strange - very strange. Apparently, Elvis was now playing with *You were always on my mind*, because, quite simply, she always was. He moaned that he didn't even like Elvis but could not get him out of his head no matter how much he tried.

I began to try to avoid him. He was draining. But avoidance was an impossibility. I woke in the morning - he was there. I went to bed - he was there. I looked in the mirror - he was there. I couldn't shake him off. There was only one topic of conversation - her.

Things were soon to get worse - much worse. She wasn't interested, and he was "free-falling toward the depths of despair." That was unfortunate because it's a long and tedious fall. I was at the communal sink cleaning my teeth one morning and saw him in the mirror complaining that this girl must be crazy not to like him, as he was good looking and had a half-decent personality - what was her problem? But she wasn't the crazy one. The *problem* was that he had met her, and since then appeared to have undergone a personality transplant, from articulate and witty to something bordering on gibberish and insane.

Apparently, U2 were now playing. This man was a walking radio. It was the song *One* with Bono singing that line about - *did I ask too much, more than a lot, you gave me nothing now it's all I got.* He didn't like U2 either. It was relentless. It all sounded like a bad acid trip in a music shop. I was becoming sick of him, but he just would not leave me alone.

"Pink Floyd play Bangalore" was the headline in some newspaper. India's hippest city seems to attract old has-been western artists for some reason. In their heyday, he had quite liked that band, but yet again he complained. He complained that a twelve-hour sleepless train journey to get to Bangalore in dusty, dirty sleeper class was the last thing he wanted. He can never sleep on Indian trains with lights being switched on and off all night, crying babies, Indian men seemingly competing with one another in the throat-clearing stakes with their endless rasping, and tea vendors crying *Chai! Chai! Chai!* along the corridors and from the platforms of every station passed through at all hours of the night. It was the sound and light show from hell.

"Why would anyone want to be woken at three in the morning for a cup of tea?" he groaned.

Anyone who has ever travelled on an Indian train could identify with the *chai* thing. One man comes along carrying a tea urn. You can hear him from the other end of the carriage. So you are left in no doubt that he is on his way. Each one sounds the same. It is a deep-throated high-pitched scream. I swear that there must be a voice training school for them somewhere on the outskirts of Delhi. Anyway, after bellowing their way through the carriage, causing the utmost annoyance, they stop and look at you, and in their normal voice ask "*Chai?*" It is as if they think you are stone deaf and have not heard them as soon as they came onto the train. And after one goes another arrives; then another; and another. Good

God, how much *chai* do they think a person needs? It is like you have died, only to be resurrected into some tedious, never ending Monty Python sketch. And I wouldn't mind if it was decent tea, but it is not. They must destroy it by putting about four spoons of sugar into each small plastic cup. For a country that grows so much tea, Indian Railways does not seemed to have conquered the art of making a decent pot yet.

Anyway, the way things were going, I was never going to get rid of this guy. And I was never going to be able to shut him up: "The worse thing is the toy sellers who try to get parents to buy tacky plastic guns or some other ear-splitting contraption for their kids. Yes, you just want to have some kid playing with that kind of thing all night!"

When the morning comes, he awakes with bags under his eyes, bags beneath the bags, hair matted with dust and feeling totally filthy. What makes it even more frustrating is that Indians get up after a perfect sleep, without a hair out of place, and are ready to go to work for the next eight hours. The first thing he does is check into the nearest hotel to sleep for the next nine hours.

He continued, "The last time I was on a train, some Indian guy eats this massive rice-meal, takes off his shoes, climbs onto the top berth and I don't see him for another twelve hours. I just hear him snoring away in some kind of *chapatti*-induced coma. He did not even come down to answer a call of nature. This is despite the non-stop yelling, crying and flashing lights. He gets down a few minutes before his station looking as right as rain and raring to go. Why can't I do that?"

Before I knew it, Indian hotels were on the agenda.

"Why is it that as soon as I check into a hotel that within five minutes I want to check out? I'll tell you why - because in half the places I stay in there is ongoing repair work taking place. The hammering and banging begins at six in the morning and carries on until eleven at night."

He also told me that any repair work did not seem to have any impact on the state of a hotel. He was useless as a craftsman, and said that too many hotel rooms looked as though he had done the repair work with paint flaking from the walls, bits of electrical wire protruding everywhere and wonky fittings: "You would think that I'd been appointed to do all of the repair work in all of the hotels in India," he said half-jokingly.

If there is a world championship for complaining, he would win it; I had no doubt. Why on earth had he come to India in the first place if all he did was belly-ache the whole time he was here? But he wasn't finished, "If they are not repairing the place, then they are adding another floor onto the top - a sixth or seventh floor on top of foundations that were probably laid to take three or four... And what about the boys who clean the place? They appear at your door at six in the morning wanting to clean the room. What the hell is that all about?"

So with all of that in mind - and it was a lot - he wasn't moving. Anyhow, he was embroiled in a serious addiction problem. He was in trouble. I was at the communal sink and yet again he was there. He looked awful. His eyes were sunken and he was unshaven. He was actually beginning to look like a junkie. His attitude had changed. He was mumbling and rambling about her bad points in the hope it would make him feel better. That kind of thing seldom does, and it never did.

He should have left long ago. He knew it. Even Indian trains had now become an attractive proposition. He had to get away. I really wished that he would - he was destroying me. He was sick of making proclamations of undying love. I guess that normal people don't act like that, but he wouldn't know - he was no longer one of them. I never saw him again - well, not until a few months later in New Delhi railway station.

Some time later I met the girl in question. She was walking through the mayhem they call the Main Bazaar, in Delhi. I glimpsed her through a maze of people, cows and bicycle rickshaws. I could see why she had had such a mesmerising effect back in Broadlands.

We went to a restaurant. As usual, the waiters outnumbered the customers. They hung around talking with each other. They waited and we waited. Eventually our order was taken, and then an eternity later an unfriendly waiter slams a bottle on the table and asks, "Open?"

I returned to my hotel. The hammering and banging continued into the night, resulting in bits of paint falling from the ceiling, and someone came knocking on my door at six in the morning wanting to clean the room.

One week after, I went to the railway station to say

goodbye. She was returning to Chennai. It was eleven in the evening. The *chai* sellers were already in full voice, accompanied by the incessant throat-clearing racket. I fought my way through the crowds and boarded the train to say farewell. I had always liked this girl - really liked her from the minute I first saw her back in Chennai. But now I knew that I'd never see her again. The train moved. She was gone forever. She would never know it, but I left my heart on the Tamil Nadu Express. Oh no! - that's not a song, is it? Jimmy Page kicked in... *Heartbreaker* began playing once again. HE was back. India might drive me mad, but that girl drove me insane!

The Art of Evasion
on an Indian Train

It was yet another long haul train journey. I was heading south from Calcutta and can remember passing the time (and there was a lot of it) by talking to Ramesh. He was a neatly dressed, thirty-something government employee. Like a lot of private conversations, they tend to become public property as anyone and everyone gathers to listen in. And it is guaranteed that on crowded Indian trains, a large audience will be listening in. So I have become an expert in the art of saying a lot without really saying much - a master in the art of evasion.

Outside the station was business as usual. It was sheer madness. Throngs of people were milling about, and a million vehicles were snarled up in a traffic jam of Indian proportions, waiting to get onto Howrah Bridge. After battling through the traffic in a yellow and black Ambassador taxi, I then battled through the crowds on blistered feet and arrived in coach S9 soaked in sweat and more than a little agitated. The length of Indian trains is phenomenal. It can be a mission in itself to find the right platform, but it's an even bigger one having to walk half-a-kilometre along the platform to get to your designated coach. Try doing it with heavy baggage in staggering humidity, while cutting a path through a thousand people. As the train pulled out of the station, I gulped down half of my ten-rupee bottle of Bisleri drinking water, secured my backpack to the metal hook under the bench, and settled down.

The usual flurry of activity then took place. *Chai* sellers, fruit sellers, toy sellers, cold drink sellers, and just about every type of seller imaginable passed through the carriage, shouting, wailing and bellowing. After the bedlam died down, Ramesh began to talk. The usual, "Tell me, what is your good name, sir?" was asked.

Then he said, "I am Ramesh, Bachelor of Commerce."

It was obviously important for him to let me know that he was a high status, educated man.

He then asked me what my job was - a simple everyday question, but not for me. I used to be many things, including a social worker, researcher, have dabbled in selling jewellery, writing, proof reading and am considering teaching English somewhere along the line. After a degree of hesitation I selected a job from my ever-growing list.

Next, he enquired about my age and whether or not I was married. With typical Indian directness he said, "You are not yet married at your age?"

Well, I have had relationships, girlfriends, and anyway, marriage is not as important in the West as it is in India - all part of my well-rehearsed stock in trade answers. Ramesh laughed and shook my hand. Being a man I can get away with having such seemingly lax morals.

By this stage about six or seven strangers had sat and were listening. I had to tread carefully. Things were getting intense. This guy was setting a minefield for me by bringing *God* into the conversation: "You are a Christian?" he asked, followed by "Do you believe in God?"

I waffled about being brought up as a Christian, and believing in *good* rather than God, while trying to sidestep the issue by saying that religion is not as important in Europe. The good rather than God reply is one of my *get out of jail cards*. It had worked before and it did again. It brought a beaming smile from Ramesh and everyone present nodded in agreement.

India is a highly structured society where family, gender, education and religion provide people with a strong sense of identity. Ramesh was trying to ascertain where I belonged in the scheme of things. But being from the less rigid West, my self-identity is more transient and by this stage was shifting by the minute according to the questions being fielded - or more precisely, to the *could-mean-anything* answers I was giving. If I didn't have an identity crisis before, then I was in serious danger of developing one now.

It was getting hot - very hot. Someone switched on the overhead fans to blow some warm air around. Thirteen men were now packed into berths that were supposed to seat eight.

The intensity stakes were cranked up a further notch as Ramesh asked, "Which country?"

I replied, "England."

"Very good country", he said, and someone shouted, "What do you think of India?"

I have learnt not to offer a personal opinion on anything in situations like this, but especially when faced with the *what do I think of India* thing. This issue can be hotter than a hot potato. Indian newspapers were full of stories about Hindu/ Muslim violence in Gujarat, Kashmir, religious fundamentalism, corruption, poverty and globalisation. I knew that it was wise not to be drawn into debate over such things in public, if at all possible. So I dealt my second escape card by saying, "Some things are good, some things are bad."

It worked. Most people laughed - not because it was funny, but because they live with the *bad* things on a daily basis and appeared to take comfort from the fact that a foreigner is also subjected to them. They knew what I was talking about without me having to say - endless queuing, form-filling, delays, bureaucracy and all other types of man-made madness.

Ramesh wanted to know, "What do British people at home think of India?"

This was successfully negotiated by pleading ignorance on behalf of the British public. I replied that people back home are largely unaware of what happens in India. I told everyone that the average Britisher knows little about the world beyond the confines of North America and Western Europe - and even then that's stretching it. India rarely features in the news.

Back home, "What do you want to go there for?" is the usual response said in a tone denoting *shock-horror* if I tell someone that I am going to India. What they really mean is that I shouldn't be going. Strange really, given their knowledge of India is ill-informed at worse and minimal at best. Unfortunately, people are less concerned with finding out about what is happening in the rest of the world and are more concerned about world-shattering events surrounding what Victoria Beckham (a pop "singer") had for breakfast, the latest tabloid sleazy sex scandal, or some other high class tit-bit from the all-important world of British celebrity-dom. It was half a world away from where I was but it might as well have been on a different planet.

The train pulled into a station, and the usual parade of auto-rickshaws was out in force near the entrance. It must have been early morning as I recall half of the drivers still curled up in the back seats not yet having risen from their night time slumber. A family was crouched on the platform eating rice-meals from banana leaves with their fingers. Next to them a vendor was yelling, "Omelette! Omelette! Omelette!"

A beautiful girl, no older than eighteen, wearing gold-coloured dangling earrings and a pink *sari* looked at me as the train moved off. I thought about where she could be going and who she might have been. Maybe she was off to attend some kind of function, she looked so elegant. But she was going nowhere and to many she was just a no one. The only *get-together* she would be attending was the marriage of hard work and low pay. She wrapped her *sari* around and tucked it in, then someone handed her a rag which she folded into a cushion on the top of her head, upon which someone else placed a board full of bricks. She was part of the family of labourers that had been toiling away behind her. Her beauty was incongruous with the brutality of it all, and I wondered if she would look so young and beautiful after a few more years of hard labour. I was a long way from home.

It saddened me to think that most of the great British public is led to believe that their world basks in a rosy glow, only slightly tinted by a few bogey men and rogue states, and a bit of poverty in this or that place. And I nearly forgot - a minor war here or there. But really that's all a long way away, and if it continues then good old Uncle Sam will put things right by bombing the hell out of someone. If it can't be put right in that manner then we will have comic relief, sports relief or some other back-slapping charity event to ease our guilty consciences. But an Indian train was neither the time nor place to vent my frustrations. I shut up before saying anything too incriminating. But Ramesh wanted to know more. His questions were incessant.

"What do most people in England do in their spare time?"

I had thought about replying along the lines of - Friday night drinking binges, followed by Saturday morning shopping sprees, followed by arranging some credit loan from the nearest bank. People have to spend their money on something even if they don't necessarily need or can afford the particular *something* that they spend it on.

I gazed out of the window and noticed a brightly painted

rural temple, almost identical to the previous brightly painted rural temple that we had passed ten minutes ago. This one was dedicated to Shiva. I knew this because a black stone figure of Nandi the bull, his mount, was positioned in front of the shrine.

Ramesh informed me, "That is a temple, sir."

Well, I didn't think it was a burger joint (surprisingly, you don't tend to get them in the middle of a field in rural India), but I replied, "Yes," trying to demonstrate grateful acknowledgement.

It made me think that debt has long since replaced religion in securing conformity in Britain - most people have too much to lose (or should that be too much to pay?) to rock the boat or to challenge things - even if they wanted to. But this aspect of the good old British way of life was best left unsaid. I didn't have the heart to burden anyone with such an unhealthy dose of faultfinding gloom. After all, Ramesh had told me that England is a *good* country and maybe it is. Anyhow, I didn't wish to shatter any illusions - Britain is what many want India to be - *developed*.

I don't suppose that I'm an expert on anything much, but if I am an expert on anything at all, it is in being able to regurgitate various viewpoints to prevent having to give an outright opinion of my own. I was asked about my views on development and India. So I mentioned J.K. Galbraith, the leading American economist, who is often quoted in the Indian press warning India not to dive headfirst into unfettered global capitalism. One of his classic quotes is something about the foolishness of feeding a horse strawberries, while expecting the masses to live on what comes out at the other end. It's not so much a case of the *trickle-down* effect, but the *trickle-out* effect, and the urban Indian elite seems hell-bent on devouring vast quantities of strawberries gulped down with a good old dollop of western values.

The train trundled along. Scores of women were working in the fields under the baking sun. The lower parts of their *saris* were pulled up between their legs to aid mobility. I grew tired just watching them. I don't think much had *trickled-down* to them. So much for strawberries! Everyone had laughed at the strawberry-eating horse story, but was unsure whether or not Galbraith's opinion was also mine. I couldn't possibly say.

Finally, my saviour arrived in the form of the ticket inspector, and everyone dispersed to sit in their designated seats. I had got through the last hour with admirable skill. Everyone had done a lot of listening, and I'd done a lot of talking. But was anyone any wiser about who I was at the end of it all? I wasn't. I then sat wondering whether I had turned into some slick and shady operator, deft in sidestepping issues - an opportunist, capable of ducking and diving with consummate ease. But then I came to the conclusion that I am really quite a decent and right-minded person - a typical product of Western culture. In other words, completely normal: unbalanced with multiple personalities, suffering from an identity crisis and unable to give a straight answer to a simple question.

Thank God for Sanjay Dutt!

This is a story about television and fame and begins in the unlikely setting of a humble eatery in South India. I was famished and stopped at the first street-side café or *dhaba* that I came across. It looked cheap and grotty, and it was cheap and grotty. The cook was frying pieces of something in ghee in a huge, blackened wok-type container or *karai* near the entrance. As I entered, he looked up and wobbled his head from side to side in acknowledgement, then shifted his glance back to the wok. I noticed that before immersion, the bits of food had already been fried, possibly hours or even days ago. I thought of blocked arteries and heart attacks. Maybe he was just making sure that the food had lost none of its super-saturated fat flavour.

He was wearing a T-shirt that had probably once been white. But that must have been a long time back. It was now layered with grime. His protruding belly indicated that it had seen more than its fair share of excessively fried tit-bits over the years. Strangely enough, there wasn't a bead of sweat on him. It must have been thirty-five degrees outside, but the flaming stove cranked up the temperature to about forty inside. I was dripping before entering and was now absolutely oozing. I pointed to the ceiling fan. He obliged by switching it on. I was the only customer and sat at one of the four tables. They had obviously been cleaned quite recently - no doubt with the oily rag next to the sink judging by the greasy wipe-marks.

I would not have thought it possible but the walls were covered with even more grime than he was. The floor was blanketed with dust and discarded pieces of food. Hygiene must have been a long lost concept to this man, but then again that suggests that he had discovered it in the first place. A guide book may politely describe the surroundings as having *character* or *charm*, others might say, filth and cobwebs. The mosaic of flaking paint and patches of dirt on the walls was interrupted by a board containing around ten light and fan switches, and a shrine with a model Ganesh situated on a shelf. I did not want to look at either the walls or floor for too long for fear of seeing hordes of roving insects. Eventually I did look but didn't see any. How could such a room be insect-free? That is when I got worried. Maybe that's what he was frying!

He said something to me in Tamil and guessing that he wanted to take my order I replied, "Meal."

He stared blankly. I repeated what I had said. He stared blankly. Then I added the all important "zzz" to the end of the word by saying, "Meals."

Bingo! He knew what I required straight away.

Meals is the catch-all word that usually implies rice, and various vegetable dishes and dips. I knew instinctively that there would be no bits of fried *thing* that he could slip in. I would easily detect them. He lifted a *thing* from the vat of oil, looked at me and shouted, "*Samosa?*"

I thought about cockroaches and shook my head vigorously.

A few minutes later a banana leaf was placed in front of me, which I sprinkled and wiped with water using my fingertips; then rice and various dishes were set out. As I began to eat, someone else came and sat at one of the other tables, smiled at me and said, "Good morning."

Then he said something to the cook in Tamil and turned to say, "Are you famous Hindi movie star..."

I interrupted by saying, "Sanjay Dutt."

He laughed, the cook laughed and I groaned inwardly while smiling. I must hear someone tell me that I look like the Bollywood hero Sanjay Dutt about four times a day. The person telling me always thinks that he is the first person ever to have told me. But it is a something of a rarity to be told this in Tamil Nadu. And it is very rare to be asked if I am actually Sanjay himself. As if Sanjay Dutt is going to be eating a rice meal in the kind of grot-shop that

I was in. Anyhow, the Tamil-speaking world has its own film industry centred in Chennai, and Sanjay or Bollywood are not as big in Tamil Nadu as they are in other parts of India. Alas, on this particular occasion, Tamil Nadu provided little sanctuary.

If I had ten rupees for every time that someone has said that I look like Sanjay Dutt then I would be as rich as Sanjay Dutt. Apparently, according to half of the Indian population, I look like him. There may be a slight resemblance, but surely not enough to merit the almost constant barrage of "You look like the famous Hindi movie star..." The only other occasion when someone asked if I was him, as opposed to just saying I looked like him, was on a platform whilst boarding a sleeper train. There was as much likelihood that Sanjay would be travelling in an ordinary second class sleeper as there was that he would be eating in a street café in Thanjavur.

I suppose being told that I look like a film star should be flattering. If I was told that I looked like Brad Pitt or Mel Gibson back in the UK then it would no doubt feel good. Unfortunately, feeling flattered is a phase long since gone. The Sanjay thing has become rather tedious and my response is now accompanied with an inner sigh, and a smile to hide my exasperation.

In India I am famous without really being famous, yet back in England I am on TV everyday. I walk down the road - I am on screen. In the railway station, I am on screen. And in every shop on the high street - yes - I am on screen. Some people would give their right arm to be on TV, but not me. I am not talking about the type of

TV that everyone watches in comfort or for entertainment, but the kind where someone gets paid to monitor and evaluate your every move. I'm talking about Closed Circuit TV. The almost ubiquitous arm of *law and order* that has found its way into every nook and cranny of public life in the UK.

CCTV came into its own when people's rights were being stripped away in the name of producing a *flexible* and *cost-effective* workforce. The legacy has been a permanent underclass of people who cannot *pay their way*. They couldn't become fully paid up members of the consumer society - they were sacrificed on its altar. Now they are surplus to requirements, the *not really wanted generation* whose spending power is minimal. It was impossible to wall them in on their housing estates, and I guess that at one time or another this had been considered, so CCTV became the next best option. The authorities regard them as a drain on welfare resources at best and as a potential threat at worst. In order to root out the *unsavoury* elements, everyone in Britain is now on screen. We are all under suspicion. British paranoia at its finest. A case of being on screen, but without the fame.

As I scooped the last bit of rice into my mouth, I looked around the café and thought that sanitised British high streets and CCTV were a million miles from the tropical, banana leaf world of South India. And I thought that Sanjay would probably have been luxuriating in his five star world somewhere. I have all of the attention and *fame* but without the fortune or wealth. But it could be worse. I once saw a Hindi film and one of the main actors had a shaven head with great tufts of hair sprouting out from his ears. At least people do not tell me that I look like him. Or worse still, Karishma Kapoor! (A female star for those who don't know.)

Being a westerner attracts a fair share of stares in India. It is a bit of an ego boost to be looked at all the time. But the stare factor goes way above and beyond the norm for a Sanjay look alike. And the feelings of self-importance that it brings are a lot different from the negative ones associated with the gaze of CCTV in Britain. All the world has become my stage. But on which stage would I rather be? There is the Sanjay-friendly one where I can revel in pretend fame. And then there is the paranoia inducing one with life being lived through a lens. A good old slice of Bollywood pretend fame, or an unhealthy dose of British paranoia? There's no contest. Thank god for Sanjay Dutt!

Back to the Future on Triplicane High Road

There was yet another power cut, or *load shedding* as they like to call it in India. Consequently, the growl of generators filled the air, and the stench of diesel wafted upward. I was hanging over a balcony, looking out over Triplicane High Road. It was dusk in Chennai. Lumbering bullocks were pulling carts and buses were weighted down at one side with people hanging on. Cows were stationary and mopeds, cars, and auto-rickshaws were competing for space. Men were making their way to the Big Mosque in response to the call to prayers, which echoed throughout the neighbourhood. Others were making their way to wherever it was they were going while street-dwelling families were arguing between themselves. On the opposite side of the road *sari*-clad women sat selling hair flowers, and others filled plastic pots with water from a municipal wagon - Chennai's response to its perennial water shortage.

The flower sellers reminded me of a song from a more innocent time which goes along the lines of - *Someone told me there's a girl out there with love in her eyes and flowers in her hair.* The song was called *Going to California.* High above Triplicane I thought that whoever said that must have been wrong. I first heard that song when I was sixteen, filled with the innocence and hope of youth. I have been looking for years for this woman but have never found her. I found women with love in their eyes, and women with flowers in their hair, but not both together. I'm not sixteen anymore and perhaps I should abandon a false hope born of the naivety of youth. But then again I have never been to California - maybe that's the problem. She is probably out there, somewhere.

I headed down the stairs and straight into the Maharaja restaurant. It is one of my favourite places and typically South Indian with banana leaves used instead of plates, and *uttapam*, *Mysore bonda*, *idlis* and *dosas* on the menu. Supervisors were shouting orders to the staff and uniformed bare-footed boys were clearing tables by placing leftovers into large metal buckets. Waiters were scurrying around shovelling out various dishes from gleaming, smaller aluminium buckets - unlimited vegetarian *meals* for a fixed price of twenty-five rupees. As usual a sense of urgency and anticipation prevailed. A customer sits and someone approaches almost immediately to set out a banana leaf and then pour water from a metal jug into a matching shiny mug. Many things in India appear inefficient and bogged down with lethargy or bureaucracy, but not South Indian restaurants - they are electrifying.

I sat next to my friend. She was elegant; she was beautiful; she was Lise. And every time I was with her I felt like melting. But this time it was different; I almost did. She had a flower in her hair! One of the boys would have been ordered to wipe me up. It would have been embarrassing to say the least to have been carried off in a bucket. She sat talking about her day, and I sat thinking about just how gorgeous she looked. Eventually the melt down phase passed and I pulled myself together.

She told me that Copenhagen is the third most expensive city in Europe to live in after London and Paris. I told her that where I live is one of the cheapest - Liverpool. I looked at one of the boys clearing the tables, and thought that he would never get the opportunity to find out. At twelve I was in full-time education. At twelve, he was working at least eight hours a day, cleaning tables. He had his life in front of him. I looked at Lise and thought that she did too. She was twenty-nine. That's when it hit me - I was no longer young - and it was bothering me! I was already patently aware of this, but normally wasn't really worried by it. I usually took comfort from knowing that I was still *relatively* young. I could tell that it was affecting me by what I was saying to Lise:

"I try to no longer think about the past or the future, but try to live in the present. I never used to." The desperate ramblings of an aging man.

For me, it was less a case of *The Age of Tyranny*, the headline in a local newspaper, but the tyranny of age. I didn't like to think about my past - it was growing almost infinitely longer by the minute and my future was growing shorter by the second. But then I thought to myself, how is it really possible to live in the present? I can never grasp it. It departs before it arrives and is impossible to board. I guess that it's only possible to anticipate some future present, or remember some present from the past. Good God, I was beginning to sound like some English teacher obsessed with verb tenses.

Lise had an enthusiasm for her future. She made me think about where I was going - or more precisely, to where I had been. I was going somewhere when I was younger and was on my way to getting there. In fact, I had got there and then decided to go somewhere else - India. I guess by the time we reach a certain age, we are told that we are supposed to be where we set out to be in our early twenties. The trouble is that I never really knew where I wanted to be, or who I was. I knew who I was supposed to be but didn't want to be it. I came to the conclusion some time ago that I'm drifting, shifting, and fluid - a kind of general multi-purpose generator oil that fits in everywhere, but has no specific purpose. Maybe the diesel fumes from outside were beginning to affect me.

I sort of ended up by accident or fate in India, talking to a Danish girl with a flower in her hair. That was the *present* and I wanted it to last forever. There was a fleeting moment in the Maharaja restaurant when she may have been that girl with love in her eyes and flowers in her hair. But we were in India, not California and we no longer live in an age of innocent hope. As usual the present was all too fleeting. Permanency is elusive.

A few months later I was in Himachal Pradesh in North India, talking with an English girl called Lisa (it was a time for Lisas or Lises - same name really). I was in a village called Vashisht and spent my birthday there. It's a beautiful place, surrounded by gentle hills and soaring snow-capped Himalayan peaks. There can be few better places in which to grow older officially. Lisa was thirty-four. She wasn't in her twenties and because of that I once again felt relatively young. When I'm fifty I'll still feel relatively young. That is until I meet someone in their twenties or by then, in their thirties, and it will be a case of me feeling relatively old. It's a strange feeling - I'll never simply be just young or old.

What of the future? When I get back to England, I will write a story. I will sit in front of the computer, alone. And because I'll be alone, I'll neither feel young nor old; I'll just be me. I will be in Cumbria surrounded by timeless misty rolling hills, and I'll look out at those English peaks and think of the poets who immortalised that amazing part of the world with their poetry. The Cumbrian Mountains, Wordsworth and Coleridge will inspire me to write about… what?… Triplicane High Road, generator oil, and *uttapams*!?

But more aptly, I will be inspired to write of things to do with love, loss and hope. And my thoughts will drift toward another time, another place - to beautiful Vashisht, the exotic Maharaja restaurant, and to a girl I once knew who had love in her eyes and a flower in her hair. I will be in the future, wanting to be back in the past, yearning for a present that never was. And I will come to the earth-shattering conclusion that the present is always absent and its absence is always present. Then I'll put on *Going to California*, listen to the soft melody, and drift away. *Someone told me there's a girl out there…* maybe I'll find her again one day in some far off land for a while - at least for a few temporary, vanishing moments. Maybe that's about all any of us can hope for.

Thirteen Hours to Midnight

They say that cricket is the biggest thing in India and I can see why it is so big. Much of it involves waiting. It is a slow paced game; chess on grass. On almost every strip of waste ground, young boys play cricket. They wait - for the bowler to bowl; for the batsman to bat; and for the fielder to eventually field. This near eternity of waiting mirrors just about everything else that goes on around them.

Napoleon once said that Britain is a nation of shopkeepers. He should have visited India today. Small one-room shops abound, specialising in just about anything imaginable. Look into each one and you will see faces gazing out into the street. They look and wait… and wait. Owners, or the relatives of owners, sit behind desks in charge of the cash. Employees watch and wait for custom. Armies of boys and men stand and wait in cafés. Many have travelled from half-way across the country to work for sixty or seventy rupees per day waiting on tables. Some work seven days a week and perhaps are allowed a few weeks off each year so they can visit their parents or wives and children.

Living in on the premises or in nearby accommodation is the norm for many, while others are given the dubious luxury of sleeping on the tables which double as beds once the restaurant closes. Their world is their job. Working for thirteen hours a day, every day, with maybe an hour break is not unusual. And midnight is finishing time. They spend their lives waiting for midnight.

Flurries of activity occur at meal times or when women come out to shop with daughters or spouses in the evening. The rest of the time is the waiting game. Just like cricket. Boring? Many would say so, but by no means all would.

"No, I do not get bored, sir. It is my duty."

This response was provided by a train attendant who had been plying the Jodphur to Allahabad route for over thirty years. His job was to attend to the needs of his passengers in a first class coach - providing pillows, allocating designated berths and such like. In Hinduism, devotion to service is regarded as a kind of devotion to God through doing the best according to your station in life.

I am not a cricket fan. I find it boring to watch, and when forced to play at school, boring to play. So it comes as little surprise to me that I get easily frustrated by India. The place is cricket with a billion people. Waiting in a queue for an hour to buy a train ticket; waiting for trains that are over three hours late; and waiting... and waiting. It does not seem to try the patience of too many Indians, whereas mine snaps all too often.

So when my friend Shweta said that she would meet me in a *dhaba* at ten-thirty in the morning, being an impatient Westerner I actually believed that she would be there. She arrived thirty-five minutes later, blaming the traffic and the cycle-rickshaw man for getting lost. But in all honesty, I was used to waiting at that stage and thirty-five minutes wasn't too bad. It could have been much longer.

Shweta was beautiful. When she walked, she glided with her *dupatta* flowing behind. She was studying for her doctorate - something to do with the history of the Indian novel. She explained it to me once. It all sounded impressive. Unfortunately, that was about the only time that she said anything to me that consisted of more than three consecutive utterances. Trying to get her to talk was like waiting for a second rate batsman to hit a six - it rarely happens. So every time I was with her the conversation was one-sided. I probed, prompted, provoked and used just about every social skill to get her to talk, but with little or no success. After a few days I almost gave up. Long periods of silence were punctuated with a remark or question from me. One word or one phrase utterances were provided in response if I got lucky. Often, it was just a smile.

When I met her she told me that her *local guardian* would be coming along shortly. I nodded trying to demonstrate a kind of knowing agreement while thinking to myself, "What the hell is a local guardian!?" It did not take long for me to find out. He was her brother's friend who was to accompany us almost everywhere we went - her chaperone. I don't suppose that it was the case that her family thought I could not be trusted with her; more the case that it may look bad for her to be seen out and about with a Western man in such a provincial town as Allahabad. I knew this because on those occasions we were chaperone-less, a few men uttered something to her in Hindi. I asked whether they had said bad things to her; she replied "Yes."

Shweta told me that her family nickname was *Lovely*. I could see why. She had a good nature. But I could not help thinking that her gentleness was in part a result of her having been more or less under the strict control of the men in her family. She came from a very traditional background. Subordination can sometimes result in a certain type of *loveliness* - the type Western women lost a long time back as they began to assert their rights.

I first met Shweta on a train going across northern India and had just laid out my bedsheet on the lower berth with the aim of settling down for the night. She was sitting opposite with her mother and father. I was quite taken aback when she initiated a conversation with me. A young Indian woman does not often begin talking to strangers, particularly foreign men. We ended up exchanging addresses and wrote to one another when I returned to England. It was a strange train ride really. Shweta and her parents alighted at around nine thirty only for another entourage to fill their place.

A man in uniform holding a machine gun sat with two quite rough-looking slightly built men. I guessed that the one in the uniform was a policeman. One of the others began to talk to me in broken English. After answering the usual array of questions put to me, he mentioned something about the Chief Minister of Uttar Pradesh. Uttar Pradesh was the state that we were travelling through and is India's most populous.

He gibbered on for a while and I exclaimed, "You are the Chief Minister of Uttar Pradesh!?"

He smiled, gave a head wobble, and fanned out his moustache with the ends of his fingers, using both hands.

My exclamation came about because I could not believe that such a scruffy figure, wearing tatty clothes and with flip-flops on his feet could be a chief minister of any state in any country anywhere on the planet. I probed just to make sure. His English was bad but I thought that perhaps he could understand what I was saying a lot more than I could understand him. Each time I quizzed him over it, he either said "Yes" or wobbled his head. What on earth would the Chief Minister of Uttar Pradesh be doing in an ordinary second class sleeper talking to some foreigner. The guy lacked any air of sophistication and I would not have trusted him to administer a drinking session in a brewery based on what I was seeing.

So out of disbelief, I pulled out my camera and said, "Photo?"

As I brought the camera to my face all three sat erect, fanned out their handlebar moustaches and put on their most serious faces. In India, it often seems to be the case that the bigger the moustache is, then the more important the wearer is. As far as photography goes, having your picture taken can be a very serious business. Many Indians forget to smile with the outcome being rather miserable looking people frowning into the lens.

A few minutes later, one of the three men mentions the word *bodyguard*. The penny drops. These three sorry figures are the bodyguards of the Chief Minister who I then find out is in the next carriage, no doubt bodyguardless as his men seem more fascinated with me than concerned for his safety. The two men not in uniform pull out their concealed weapons to show me. It was unnerving to think that these two had formal legitimacy for carrying guns. Their whole demeanour and attitude seemed totally amateur.

An official from the Chief Minister's carriage comes along and the three men disappear with him. The only thing to remind me that they had been with me is the cumbersome looking machine gun on the opposite bench, which the uniformed guy just happened to forget. About thirty seconds later he reappears and collects it as if he was just returning to pick up a newspaper that he had forgotten to take with him. I suppose that he did not think it careless to have left it with a complete stranger, probably believing that it would have required a good ten minutes for me to stare at the thing and wait... and wait, before finally deciding to pick it up and spray mayhem throughout the Chief Minister's carriage.

The next morning the train crawled into New Delhi station. Over the next nine days I do a lot of staring and waiting. I stare at the ceiling as I wait in bed lying flat on my back. I make frequent visits to the bathroom and stare down the toilet as I throw up into it. It is Christmas and New Year time and I am stuck in the hotel Vishal nursing a severe bout of dysentery. It is one of the coldest periods on record in Delhi. At night the temperature falls to five degrees. People walk around wrapped in blankets or shawls with their breath clouding the night air. When Indian cities are cold and cloudy they can be very depressing. The filth, power cuts and chaos seem more salient. At least when bathed in sun, they appear more appealing.

Over the nine day period that I am laid up in bed with the Bob Segar version of *Santa Claus is Coming to Town* constantly bellowing from a room across the hallway, the Kashmiri occupant and his German girlfriend are stuck in Delhi waiting to head north into the mountains. Every time I think of Bob Segar or hear that song, I automatically think of dysentery. I am sure that Bob Segar wanted to be remembered for so much more. After I recovered, I took a forty-hour train journey south to Chennai. I needed a warmer climate. A few days after arriving, I take a plane back to the UK. I had had a gutful of India - literally.

A few months later, I returned to see Shweta. And a few months after that I never saw or heard from her again. I suppose that I got sick of waiting - waiting for her to be someone she wasn't - waiting for her to become someone she couldn't be. It was all my fault. In some ways Shweta was a product of her country. I should not have expected her to change. In India, you wait, you accept, and you take things as they are. It is all like a game of cricket. Much of the waiting in India is punctuated with remarks from well-intentioned people who say, "Take a seat. You drink *chai*?" As if sitting and drinking tea will make it all OK. It will not, but it is all part of the game.

I am writing this after having finished a ten-hour coach journey. Every journey begins in the same manner. The guy who packs the bags into the storage compartment of the bus slams it shut and frantically cajoles everyone to get on board. The driver has started the engine. Everyone rushes to get on in a state of semi-panic thinking that departure is imminent. But alas, it never is. We then sit waiting for about half-an-hour. We wait for the last passenger to arrive, for the driver to get his time sheet filled in or God knows what, why or who. And me? I usually end up on the wrong side of the bus with the sun blazing down and sweating buckets.

On arrival I checked into a hotel. After lying on my bed for twenty minutes I feel that I am getting bitten. I am. I look at the sheets and find about half a dozen bed bugs. I go to see the manager at the reception.

"I pay one hundred rupees for bed bugs," I complain.

He looks at me in a way that says - "So what is your problem?"

After waiting and thinking, he finally says in a polite manner, "Yes sir, but there are not that many."

I try to explain that it only requires one bed bug to get eaten alive. Again he waits and thinks. Eventually he tells me to wait in my room and one of the hotel boys will be along to sort it out. After forty-five minutes, one of his boys arrives with a bulky contraption strapped to him. He points the nozzle of the tube at the bed and sprays some foul smelling stuff on the sheets. I started to cough and have to leave the room. The manager comes along and tells me that all will be OK in ten minutes after the fumes go. Eventually they did. After ten hours.

I never did get to like cricket. And it is probably going to be a long haul for me to get to like India. But I have been there for long enough and visited so many times. I have spent years rather than months in the place. Maybe it's time I packed up my bat and ball and went home. Cricket was never any fun.

The Point of No Return: Love and Death in India

I suppose that men cannot really describe other men as being *sweet*. Someone I once knew in India, a woman, liked to call certain men sweet, but I never felt that I could. But Sach was sweet. He had a gentle nature, a particular sweetness. Some people may be described as being likeable, but Sach was more than that. He was the sensitive type.

I had not long arrived in Delhi after having spent four months in Chennai, and was on the Main Bazaar, the big traveller hangout, when I met Sach in the courtyard of the Shiva Hotel. I sat next to him and asked Mr Kahn, the in-house *chai-wallah*, for some tea. Sach began to talk. He was second or possibly third generation British-Asian, and had been travelling in India for quite some time. India was intended to be part of his big world trip that would eventually take him to South America. That had been his plan before leaving England, but things had changed. He would never leave India.

Sach looked like any other traveller who had been on the road for a while. He was unshaven with straggly hair, and wore the usual traveller-friendly hippy type gear. Sach had met a French woman earlier in his trip. He had fallen in love with her, and she with him - or so he thought. It was to be no short-term, superficial traveller fling. But six months into the relationship, when they were together in Hampi, she woke up one morning and told him that she had had enough. It was out of the blue. Sach had been devastated. He still was. But there was more. She was pregnant and when I met him was about to have his baby. He told me that he was about to be a father, yet did not know where his ex-girlfriend was. She could have been in India, France or just about anywhere. He had lost her. She was gone forever.

Sach told me that he had given his all to this woman. He was the type who would have wanted it that way. He was a highly sensitive person. I suspect that being *in love* or falling *in love* can mean different things to different people. Sach struck me as the all or nothing type. As I sat listening I thought about *love* and pondered that at one stage he may have told her that he would give her everything he was - his love, his onliness, his selflessness. Those are my words and feelings, not his. But if he did not actually say this, then I thought that surely he must have felt it. Perhaps Sach both felt and said all of those things in his own way, in his own words.

I could not help but feel sorry for him. And I thought that after his girlfriend had left, he may have gazed out of his hotel window each night, wherever he was, and looked mournfully into the street, across the hills or down onto the plains, wondering where on earth she was, all the time trying to recall her voice, her laughter, her smile. Did he still call her name? Did he wonder if his would ever pass her lips again? I don't know. Possibly none of that happened - but going by events about to unfold, I'm almost certain that it did.

Sach's father had just died and he was trying to get back to the UK in time for the funeral. His money was running out. I guess he had almost spent what was intended to be two years worth of travelling money in just over six months. Such is love. He was having no luck. All of the flights back home had lengthy waiting lists. He could not get home. To make things worse, even if he did get back, he was twenty thousand pounds in debt to various banks. He had little incentive to work if a large slice of his earnings was to go straight into paying off his debts. I do not know how it works, but I suspect that the banks would have some legal claim to a large part of his salary. Part of the reason for his trip seemed to be to escape his debts. One of the last things he asked was whether I knew of any informal cash-in-hand work in England. I didn't.

I met Sach on one other occasion only. The next day he was sitting in a street café on the Bazaar. He looked down; even more so than the day before. He was resigned to the fact that he would not be able to get home in time for the funeral, and told me he planned to go in to the mountains to buy hashish to sell to foreigners in Goa. It was not really a plan. It was a half-hearted fumble to try to salvage something from the wreckage of things. Deep down, he probably knew it.

You never really know how low a person might be feeling. And Sach was low - very low. He was young, had tearful deep brown puppy dog eyes, was personable, and had a certain positive magnetism that still managed to flicker despite his depression. I could see it and I could feel it. He seemed to be one of those people who had been in love with life - and with some French woman as well. But the next day I was to find out that all of his positive attributes did not account for much.

Sach had lost faith, belief and hope. He wanted a better tomorrow and almost anything would have been better than the day he was living. Sach was on the trip of a lifetime - he would make no other like it. Two days later he was dead. Someone told me that a foreigner had been found hanging from a ceiling fan in a hotel a few doors away from mine. His name was Sach. He committed suicide. Five thousand miles from home, alone and lost. He ended his life in some faceless hotel room on the Main Bazaar in Delhi. He must have shed a thousand tears onto the marble floor in that room. Then again, he may possibly have had none left at that point. He was by no means the first to end his life on that street. Over the years there were always tales of some foreigner committing suicide in this or that hotel.

A few months earlier, during late 2001, the former Beatle George Harrison died. He had his ashes flown to India and some were scattered on the Ganges near Varanasi. George had great affinity with India and its belief systems. He was a Hare Krishna devotee and was usually described as a *gentle* man - even a *sweet* man. He came from my home town, and like me, had grown up to the sound of seagulls and foghorns from the ships on the River Mersey. Because of our common birthplace and the fascination with India, I felt something inside me when he passed away although I had never met or known him. His death was widely reported in the Indian press. Everyone will remember George. He was famous. He did not die alone among strangers in some characterless backpacker haunt. Suicide on the Main Bazaar is no way to die. I had known Sach and also felt something inside when I heard that he had died - but what I felt this time was much deeper.

Before he reached Delhi, the final destination, Sach had been to Rishikesh - the place where George Harrison and the rest of the Beatles visited in the 60s. Out of all the Beatles, George Harrison gained most inspiration from this encounter with Indian mysticism by returning to the UK to write songs, play the sitar and to develop his beliefs. It could not have been more different for Sach. He did a Reiki course while in that town. He told me that one night in his room he experienced a *visitation*. A figure entered the room, whispered his name and disappeared, yet he felt her presence for some time next to him as he lay on the bed. It was a bad presence, according to Sach. He was obviously unnerved by it all. India does strange things to people. It can inspire and create dreams.

It did so for George Harrison. In a different way, it also did for Sach. And the small town of Rishikesh appeared to have had a big impact upon both of their lives.

What happens when dreams shatter into pieces and are blown into the gutter where no one gives a damn? Sach chased an illusion, a bright but elusive rainbow. It faded to nothing. He was still in love when he died, still shackled by emotion and unable to fall out of love. To see through an illusion and walk out of it the other side takes time. Suicide ends the potential for that.

Sach died five months ago. He was not famous; he was not a millionaire; he did not come from my home town. He probably did not even get a mention in the local Delhi newspapers when he died. But every time I find myself on the Main Bazaar I at least think of him. I also think of his poor mother who lost her husband and then her son. Maybe she never got to hear his story. Perhaps she was informed only that he had committed suicide. I don't know if he left a note or had spoken to her. And I don't know if I was the last person or only person who he opened his heart to. Sach was sweet. A young man with the hopes and dreams of youth. This story is in memory of him. Some may say that suicide is selfish and for the weak. I disagree. There is little without love, and even less without hope.

Time Travel on
the Road to Nowhere

I lay on my bed reminiscing about 1960s Northern England where I lived as a child. It must have been about midnight and I thought about streets full of terraced houses, factory chimneys rising in the distance down by the docks, and rag and bone men crying, "Any old iron?" in sing-song wailing voices as they pushed their carts along the roads. Of course, there were also people: parents, family, and friends. Nearly all of those old working class streets have gone the way of the bulldozer, and the people - while most are still alive, a few are long dead.

The relentless ticking of my miniature alarm clock penetrated the silence as my thoughts then drifted toward where I was - India. Images began to flood my mind in the form of temple elephants, roadside vendors, film music, and power cuts. I could see foamy mouthed bullocks pulling carts, sky-high kites being flown by children from rooftops in Delhi or in blue-walled Jodphur, and *puja* being offered on the banks of the Ganga. Then there was the almost silent air-conditioned swishness of Spencer Plaza on Chennai's Anna Salai (Spencer's is India's biggest shopping mall). As I lay half-asleep, half-awake it was clear that they had their own unique resonance; some obvious and abrasive, others more subtle and lilting. Nonetheless each possessed a certain commonality - they were the sound of the present.

I thought of the Taj Mahal in Agra, the Sun Temple at Konark, the Vijayanagar ruins at Hampi, Bodhgaya where Buddha achieved enlightenment, and the Kailasa temple at Ellora carved out of the very mountain where it sits. The full weight of history hung heavy as I lay thinking about the great monuments and sites of India. And I remembered virtually every face that I had seen on the street during the day just gone. All of what I saw, from the temple at Konark to the people on the street, had one thing in common. They were echoes from the past, products of labourers, rulers and of great-great grandparents now long gone.

The echoes grow louder with time. The further into the past people and places become, the sharper the significance and memories of them are. Phrases uttered by people no longer alive or no longer known, now seem more haunting and clearer. The expressions of history, manifested through palaces, monuments or the dull, grey streets of Northern England, appear more significant and meaningful than they ever did before. And because the reverberations of the past are stronger, the appreciation of the present is greater. Maybe, I have just learnt to listen harder.

When I step foot on the street once more, in front of me will be a kaleidoscope of brightly coloured *saris, dupattas,* decorated holy cows, and all of the paraphernalia that I associate with India - with the *other,* with what is different to what I once knew. But then I will turn around and look toward my past, and realise that it has caught up with the present and hitched a ride to India. It will not be such a heavy burden though. In fact, it will make the journey that much more interesting than it would have been than if I had travelled with youth alone.

For some who travel, the experience is all about seeing the sights, mentally (and sometimes physically) ticking them off some list, and all accomplished within a fixed timescale. I have met people who adopt this approach and then tell me that they have now *done* this or that country. It all seems a bit too calculated, suffocating and tedious. Through memory, the past is always present; and through our constant anticipation of it, so is the future. Whereas the past can be a comforting companion, for some the future - the unknown - can be filled with dread if there is nothing to control it. So what better way to constrain the future (and to dull the present) than to adhere to a highly rigid and predefined travel itinerary? It is the safe way to *travel,* a kind of second-hand sanitised version where a true sense of exploration is lost. And people become disengaged from the present through having sacrificed it to the future.

Travel is freedom. The spirit of travel is not about getting from one physical point to another, but about embarking on the road to nowhere - a future shrouded in mystery. When this happens, the future seems open and inviting, and the present is no longer closed but engaging. No physical end-point is required; just a willingness to live in the here and now. Time implies a future and past, but really, there is neither - only the now. And travel should be about the now - what takes place in the present. It is all a state of mind. The past and future are virtual reality. The present is all we have, soaked with echoes from the past and electrified by anticipation of the future. So the aim is to make the most of it by letting yourself be transported to somewhere else, somewhere different in time, space, body and mind. It can be a difficult place to get to, but that is the aim of many a traveller.

16

Pancake Overload

"Are you telling me that travelling is a complete waste of time?"

Jan was a wide-eyed backpacker from New Zealand who couldn't quite believe what I was saying. He was *doing India* by journeying along the well-worn banana-pancake circuit. He had his set-list of places to visit and things to see - because the guide book said he must, and was probably ticking them off with a pen and gained immense satisfaction from having done so.

He began his day early, clutching his book (and pen), and returned hours later (still clutching book and pen) after having gone through his tick-list, and having achieved his daily quota of sights.

I answered his question in a somewhat tongue-in-cheek manner by saying, "Yes, that's about it. Look at the banana-pancake circuit. It's just an endless stream of westerners passing through the so-called hotspots of India on their way to nowhere in particular."

I could see that I was having the required shock effect as intended, and so continued by saying, "They spend a few days in a once-in-a-lifetime must-see spot, and then move on to the next once-in-a-lifetime must-see spot. They seek permanent excitement and pleasure, but after a while it all means nothing to them. Excitement and pleasure are best served in small and temporary doses, otherwise they become meaningless."

The banana-pancake circuit is mediocrity in purest form. It is a safe trail of easy-to-see places, and relatively few backpackers venture beyond the confines. This is disappointing as some of the best places and better experiences are to be found beyond. The pancake trail is *lowest common denominator travel,* the easily digestible route for the mass backpacker in transit, and the Lonely Planet guide book is one of the books unwittingly responsible for creating or sustaining the phenomenon. In William Sutcliffe's classic *Are you Experienced?* the Lonely Planet guide is referred to as *the book*, the bible for backpackers - and that's the problem. Too many unimaginative travellers treat it as the definitive word in travel.

The pancake-circuit consists of towns or areas within cities that have hotels and cafes aimed almost exclusively at foreigners - and banana, chocolate, honey and any other form of pancake you can think of is usually listed on the menu. It's quite strange really, because in my entire life, I've never seen a banana pancake on a menu in any place back home, and what's more, had never eaten one before I came to India.

Pushkar, Manali, Udaipur, Hampi, parts of the Main Bazaar in Delhi, and particular streets in Varanasi form part of the circuit. They are all listed in *the book* (and other books beside), and are great places to hang out and meet other westerners. They tend to make the travel experience in India more bearable. But many become trapped in these traveller ghettos. They have become popularised by the guide books, and are a sanitised world developed for foreigners. Too many pass through like headless chickens.

I was talking to Jan in a pancake-type street café in Mamallapuram, a dusty, sun-baked coastal town about 50 kilometres south of Chennai. He continued to listen to my rant - "After two or three days in a "must-see" location, a lot of backpackers get bored of the place, their own company, or of other backpackers. They feel compelled to move on believing that the next hot-spot will be better than the last, and the people there will be more interesting."

Their journey continues in a self-delusory mode, because as soon as people get to where they think they want to be, many realise that they didn't want to be there in the first place or at least want to be somewhere else - somewhere better. The problem is that some seek a permanent high from *doing the circuit.*

Jan was probably thinking what I was thinking about myself - "What's this guy doing here if he feels like this? Why doesn't he do us all a favour and go home."

If he was, he was too courteous to have said it. He countered by saying, "What about those people who come here and spend weeks or even months in one spot, doing courses on meditation, yoga or something like that? They can't be described as running around like headless chickens."

That was the cue for me to whine about one of my favourite topics - "A lot of those types are trying to find themselves. I always wonder where on earth did they lose themselves. If they had lost themselves in England, then that would be the place to search. Why come half way across the world? And if they had indeed lost themselves, then who are they now? If they don't know, then who does? They are completely bananas - a case of pancake overload."

Jan was on his first big trip away from home. He was overwhelmed by India - well at least by what he was seeing of it - the palaces, forts, and temples along with the everyday chaos and colour that bombard you in the streets. Give him a couple of months and *temple-fatigue* will have set in. He won't have reached my heady standards by then, but he'll be on his way - perhaps.

My attitude was the end product of an eight-month trip and I had been out too long. Ten trips to India in as many years would place a strain on the most ardent of traveller; and it had. It was time to leave. I went to Chennai to the main tax office to obtain a tax clearance certificate. This form supposedly proves that you have not been working in India during your stay. It's a useless piece of paper really, because no one has ever asked me for it on leaving India. But I thought it was best to be safe than sorry.

On the fume-belching bus from Mamallapuram to Chennai, I must have had two or three separate conversations with local people. Each one was the same.

"What is your good name, sir?" - "How old?" - "Married?" - "What is your job?" and so on; a mind-numbing daily question-and-answer ritual based around my status.

So I was happy to find something different when I got to the tax office - the one place more than anywhere else where you would expect to be asked such questions. Tax offices are foreboding places - officialdom (*babudom*, to borrow an Indian term) running riot, but I was pleasantly surprised. I entered the room designated for foreigners and there she was - a cow of a woman (in the nicest possible sense, of course). Many women in India remind me of the street cows found in every town and city. They stand exuding serenity, surrounded by urban chaos, and have a certain understated dignity. They glide along almost unaffected by the brutality of the urban world, and possess a certain presence that western women tend to lack.

The tax officer in question engaged me in the longest conversation that I'd had with an Indian woman in eight months (or should that be, the only conversation?). That probably says less about my social skills and more about the general position of women in India. It was the most interesting and unusual encounter I'd had for a long time. This was a woman who didn't care to engage on a trivial level. She was deep.

She compared the nature of patriarchy in India with elsewhere, and talked about the petty vindictiveness of bureaucrats (*babus*). I suspected that her expertise on these matters stemmed from first-hand experience, and was the result of her having been a casualty of both on a daily basis. Then she surprised me by talking about, of all things, permanency and disillusionment. She told me that we all seek permanency in our lives, but as soon as it seems to appear we want something else. So everything is just temporary. Even disillusionment is temporary - intermittently peppered with moments of happiness (perhaps not, as it always comes back to haunt).

I realised her expertise on this subject was probably also based on first-hand experience. It was perhaps the result of her having seen and spoken with so many jaded western backpackers who had passed through her office over the years. This was a woman after my own heart. She was enchanting. I got the impression that she wanted to be somewhere else, but felt trapped forever inside tax office hell or *babudom*. The most frustrating thing was that she knew it, and couldn't do anything about it.

I left rickshaw-choked Chennai clutching my tax certificate and headed to Delhi to fly home. After a thirty-six-hour train journey, I arrived totally shattered and checked into a hotel. It was full of westerners bloated with pancakes. I read my Lonely Planet guide and pondered about the permanency of disillusionment, the "temporariness" of happiness, the disillusionment of permanency, and the happiness of temporariness. It was an absolute nightmare. I decided to go to sleep. I suddenly felt enclosed, and woke up sweating and gasping for breath. I had dreamt that I was trapped forever inside a giant banana pancake. The most frustrating thing was that I am; I know it, and can do little about it. No matter how much we try to escape from bland standardisation or mass conformity, it is, increasingly, the way of the world.

Internet India

I had just travelled along the Delhi to Jaipur road. It took an age to get out of the city. Delhi seemingly goes on forever. The bus fought its way through traffic jams, people, urban sprawl and more urban sprawl. As we passed the Indira Gandhi International Airport, I thought, "At last - we must be nearly out of the city." Officially we probably were. But I didn't account for the new developments. It must have been about another forty minutes before we encountered countryside.

The Delhi-Jaipur route is fascinating. It is where hi-tech India meets rural India. The edge of the Delhi conurbation is now scattered with ugly high-rise apartment blocks. I can never work out whether it is they that are grey and dismal, or it is the haze that makes them appear that way. They are too far in the distance to provide me with an answer. From the distance, they look as though they were inspired by Soviet era planning. Maybe from close up they are beautiful. I doubt it. Nearer to the road, however, is hi-tech Delhi. Office blocks gleam in their newness and would not look out of place in Manhattan or Hong Kong.

As we follow the road we eventually hit greenery. Within another hour or so we are in Rajasthan. The contrast with that part of the road that leads out of Delhi cannot be more striking. Village women walk along dirt paths close to the road, dressed in long yellow veils. They look as though they have just time travelled forward from two hundred years ago. They carry pots on their heads and are covered from head to toe with jewellery. The hardships of rural India are etched into their darkened, sun-baked faces. Tall, elegant village men dressed in white and wearing traditional headgear cycle and walk along the tarmac. This is bullock-cart India.

People in the West used to section the world according to First, Second and Third World terminology. Those are outdated stereotypes, and even then they were misguided. But in the age we live in, global corporate capitalism is everywhere. Its monuments, the shiny office blocks, are no longer as confined as they were to Western cities. To use the old terminology - the *First World* is now firmly entrenched in the *Third*. You do not have to look at the office blocks in Delhi or to survey the IT parks near Bangalore or Hyderabad to know this, but it kind of reinforces it.

So what has all of this got to do with the Internet? Well, if hi-tech India has now crawled its away along the Delhi-Jaipur road, it does not stop there. The Internet in particular is clawing its way into rural India. It is already on just about every major street in every town. Internet cafés abound. Some are nothing more than box rooms with three or four machines crammed in. From the outside the building may look like a crumbling shed on a cow-infested, muck-strewn street, but inside is the majestic PC. Others are larger enterprises, with rows and rows of machines.

These days, the Internet and computer technology are no longer confined to middle class urban dwellers. Schemes exist to give slum children access in Mumbai, and agencies such as the Swaminathan Research Foundation supports putting *knowledge centres* into villages in Tamil Nadu, close to Pondicherry. The centres have been effective in empowering rural communities with information in the fields of environment, health, sustainable agriculture and aquaculture, meteorology, markets and prices.

For example, in a coastal village inhabited by fisher families, the women download from the Internet each evening information on the likely wave heights in the sea adjoining their village at various distances from the shore line. This information is broadcast throughout the village through loudspeakers. The fishermen then have access to accurate information on sea conditions before they set out fishing in their wooden boats. "Development," if it is to mean anything, has to make the benefits of technology available to people in a way that is meaningful to them. And that does not necessarily mean encouraging Western-inspired, urban-led consumerism, whereby people become bombarded into submission in front of global TV with eyes wide shut.

I am sure there are dozens, maybe hundreds, of organisations across India attempting to bridge the digital divide with various projects. Globalisation without ethics or equity may be the unstated logo for the rich and powerful, but not seemingly for everyone. Giving rural people access to IT may not in itself bridge the cleavages between rich and poor in the world, but it is about planting a seed from which something better may grow.

Writers of the World Unite!

It was a cold and dreary January and I was in a bookshop on a high street in an English town, flicking through the pages of a travel magazine. The front page had an inviting photograph of a red sky sunset over Darwin, Australia. Splashed down the left-hand side were the feature contents for the month. It was highly polished and glossy, and arguably the kind of publication to advertise in, to write for and to be seen reading. A professional magazine for professional people. But then I woke to find that it had all been a bad dream. I was not surrounded by fabricated gloss on some faceless high street, but in a one hundred rupee a night lodge in Madurai, South India. I was across the street from the Sri Meenakshi Temple. Its soaring *gopurams* (towers) were covered in a riot of carved and vividly coloured godlike figures, and I was not freezing in bleak mid-winter, but sweltering in the heat of a tropical January.

After *showering* by using the jug and bucket method, I went along to a local Internet café to check out the website of the magazine that I had dreamt about. The submission guidelines stated that what is required are factual pieces on destinations - where to stay, what to do, costs, quality of service and so on. The magazine only publishes one traveller tale type article in each edition, but even then requires it to be less than eight hundred words. The guidelines state you have a one in eight hundred chance of being published, and that most people who appear in it will most probably be better at writing than you are. What is more, it is implied there is a good chance that they may also be better travelled! So they advise prospective candidates to think very hard before submitting.

Some may argue that the editors are being realistic - others might say, merely pretentious.

I have read the magazine in question, and yes, the standard of writing is high. But then again I've read a host of webzines on the Internet. The quality can be just as high, but, and a big but here, they provide a forum for different writing styles, and include a diverse range of approaches and opinions on travel ranging from life-changing trips to culture-shock stories, to social comment. Consequently, they are more of an interesting read. In certain magazines, traveller tales have to conform to highly specific content guidelines and provide little scope for diversity. But I suppose that they are probably more soothing and therapeutic because you can feel the glossiness of the pages and delude yourself that you are reading *high* literature because you have paid a top price for a self-labelled *up-market* mag.

It is not the intention of the editorial staff to discourage people from writing or to undermine a writer's self-belief. After all, they are caught in the competitive web of profit margins and markets. Unlike electronic publishing, print publishing can be an expensive endeavour. Although certain websites can have very specific requirements, many do not. They actually encourage writers to write. Their editorial policy states that all they require is "good quality writing." I remember when I first stumbled across various webzines. It was refreshing to have found something that offered wide-ranging opportunities for writers, and you didn't have to be an established, big name.

In the world we live in, a prevailing belief is that if something does not sell then it is no good. Or, in other words, if there is no profit in it, then it is useless. This is the error of the age. In the writing game, according to most editorial policies, your writing is not *good* enough if it cannot justify itself in terms of quantifiable sales or increased readership. Webzines have changed the rules. Many are run by dedicated individuals or teams whose financial overheads are not the same as the printed media, and who make little or no profit from what they do. They are also less constrained by considerations to do with space (number of pages). As a result, the whole process of getting published is more democratic and inclusive. You do not have to be a big name, or to write solely for the market with the aim of boosting sales.

Certain Internet sites for writers accept good quality work on a huge range of topics. There are a lot of good writers -

even exceptional ones - who can find it difficult to get into print, but have found an outlet on the Internet. Before the advent of the Internet, good quality writing and *publishable quality* were much less mutually inclusive bed-fellows. Through the Internet, more people are being published and a greater diversity of voices is being heard. Certain *glossies* lose something through their policies of exclusion. Their loss can be a webzine's gain.

The Internet has opened up a whole new world for people who write - and who write well. Just because it is electronic and not print, and there is usually no payment, does not mean that getting published in various Internet mags is in some way inferior or that the quality of writing is poorer. Good writing should be valued in itself for being interesting, pleasurable or thought-provoking, and not be evaluated solely in terms of its commodity value in the market place. Writing for the pleasure of it and because you want to say something can be rewarding, and if it earns a bit of money along the way, then even better.

The enjoyment of writing and having what you write made accessible to the public are hugely motivating in themselves. And through the Internet, access to the public has increased. Financial gain isn't everything. Those who travel-write for webzines are ordinary people, travelling on their own money and incurring all of the risks entailed with independent travel. There is no support system, financial remuneration or advantages accrued from being a big name writer or celeb. But they share something in common - having something interesting to say (sometimes a lot more interesting than the celeb writers), and saying it well in the form of the written word.

There are no camera crews, expense accounts or photographers to accompany me when I am travelling through India. I'm not Michael Palin! (Palin is a British celeb who has done a lot of travel stuff on TV). I stay in grotty hotels, eat in *dhabas* (basic hole-in-the-wall street cafés), spend days on second class Indian sleeper trains and get dysentery, down and out, exhilarated and stimulated. I am just an average traveller who spends some time in Internet cafés in India writing. By spending between ten and thirty rupees an hour for Internet use, I have become lifted out of obscurity by the Internet. From a back street Internet café in Delhi, Chennai or some back-of-beyond town in Madhya Pradesh, my world becomes published. I have something to say, have been given the opportunity to say it and hopefully someone somewhere will read it. What can be more democratic and empowering than that?

I have virtually replaced my camera with a PC and it feels great. I could never really have hoped to had got my photos published. I know next to nothing about photography and have a cheap point-and-shoot camera. Poor quality in any field should not hope to cut the mustard, but something of good quality should. Good quality writing should be published, particularly if the writer has something original to say. It should not left on some shelf gathering dust just because it cannot be commodified and falls between the cracks in the market - not appealing to strictly defined audiences who may rake in advertising revenue and whom advertisers can *target*. Now there is less chance that it will gather dust, thanks to the Internet. What is more, webzines are immediately accessible worldwide. I no longer have to be in a bad dream on an English high street - just in an Internet café somewhere in Asia.

Who knows what the Internet may do for the digital divide in the slums of Mumbai, or the villages of Tamil Nadu. But on a personal level, without the Internet, this book would never have existed. It inspired me to travel-write and to continue to write. My work became published and my self-belief flourished. Eventually, I thought that I was good enough - good enough to write a book.